The foreign policy of
Charles de Gaulle

D1000869

A

The foreign policy of Charles de Gaulle

A CRITICAL ASSESSMENT BY

Paul Reynaud

FORMER PREMIER OF FRANCE

Translated by

MERVYN SAVILL

THE ODYSSEY PRESS · NEW YORK
PAUL HAMLYN · LONDON

Published by
THE ODYSSEY PRESS, INC. New York
PAUL HAMLYN LIMITED · Westbook House · Fulham Broadway · London
English translation © 1964 by Paul Hamlyn Limited
First published in France by René Julliard under
the title *La Politique Etrangère du Gaullisme*
© 1964 by René Julliard
All rights reserved
Printed and bound in Great Britain
by Bookprint Limited, Kingswood and Crawley

Preface

FROM THE BEGINNING OF THEIR HISTORY AS A FREE PEOPLE, THE Americans have been friends of France. They have saved us from two world wars. Their Marshall Plan rescued us from economic chaos.

Since the Entente Cordiale at the beginning of this century the British have been our allies. Their valour during the First World War was unquestionable, and in the Second World War it was the English who, in the stirring words of Winston Churchill, promised a fallen France that her honour and her dignity would be restored to her.

Both Great Britain and the United States kept their word, and now they are surprised to hear France officially refuse the cooperation that is demanded of her by her allies in the common defence of Europe; to hear France attack the 'Anglo Saxons'; to have France's veto flung in their face when Great Britain applied for membership in the Common Market.

They are surprised to see France greet with mistrust the 'Kennedy round' of the tariff talks and to hear her suggest the departure of the Americans from Vietnam, when it is the Americans who have been championing the cause of the West against Communist China under the most difficult of conditions—conditions which she had already coped with in Korea.

It is essential that our American and British friends know that this policy does not speak for the opinions and the sentiments of the whole French people. They must realise that this represents the will of one man, whose motives we intend to uncover.

Paul Reynaud

Contents

CHAPTER 1 *Worn out dogma and lively resentment*

'Only great men have great faults.'
LA ROCHEFOUCAULD

GENERAL DE GAULLE HAD THE HAPPY IDEA OF BEGINNING HIS *Memoirs* with a definition of his patriotism, which throws a light on his whole future foreign and military policy.

'The emotional side of me,' he tells us, 'tends to imagine France as a fairy-tale princess . . . But the practical side tells me that France is only really herself when she is in the front rank.'

Naturally every patriot wants France to be a leader among nations. And so she can be in certain fields; in the field of morality, letters, science and the arts. But she is no longer the France of Louis XIV or of Napoleon.

How can France possibly rank with America, with her four-times greater population and her agriculture and industry which extend over a continent flanked by two oceans?

How can she compare with Soviet Russia, which since the last war extends from a point 60 miles east of the Rhine to Vladivostock on the Pacific, straddling half Europe and Asia, and whose population is even greater than that of America?

No more than Great Britain, which accepts the fact, can France hope to be in the same class as the two giants, each of whom commands an entire continent.

We shall see this fanciful notion, 'France in the front rank', leading de Gaulle on towards further illusions, causing him, in his disappointment, to adopt a hostile attitude towards our British and American allies.

The world being split in two, de Gaulle is bound to clash either with the American or the Russian giant. He pondered upon this problem in London during the war. He refused to admit that his patriotic slogan of

'France in the front rank' was unrealistic. In those days he dreamed—and he has never ceased to dream—of a France at the head of Western Europe, either containing Russia or entering into partnership with her, by creating 'Europe from the Atlantic to the Urals'. From this Europe he excludes not only America but also Great Britain, whose larger population, greater wealth and international influence need no stressing.

After the liberation of Paris: From Gibraltar to the Urals.

After the liberation of Paris, de Gaulle took up residence at the War Ministry. In Volume III of his *Memoirs* published in 1959, a year after his return to power, he reveals the ideas he nursed in 1944. Europe, he said, could only achieve stability and peace through an association of Slavs, Germans, Gauls and Latins. He admitted that there was a snag—the fact that Bolshevism had pushed its rule as far as the Vistula, the Danube and the Balkans. 'But,' was his immediate reply, 'as soon as Germany ceases to be a threat, Russian domination, deprived of its *raison d'être*, will sooner or later appear intolerable to the vassal states, while the Russians themselves will lose any desire to extend their frontiers . . . In the long run no regime can survive against the will of the people . . . Following this retraction of Communist rule, the foundations of a United Europe could be laid in the form of an organised association of these races from Ireland to Istanbul, and from Gibraltar to the Urals.

'Such was the plan I conceived . . . ' This was his dream.

After the Victory: Three solutions.

After the victory of the Allies in May, 1945, and faced with the collapse of Germany and Russo-American antagonism, de Gaulle, as he tells us in his *Memoirs*[1] began thinking of putting into practice 'the vast plan which I had conceived for my country'.

Actually, he vacillated between several contradictory plans: 'To collaborate with the West and the East, to conclude if necessary appropriate alliances with either side, while accepting no kind of dependency'.

Thus there were three possible solutions:
(1) Collaboration with the West and the East.
(2) Formation of an alliance with the West.
(3) Formation of an alliance with the East.

---

[1] *Salvation*, Volume III of *The War Memoirs of Charles de Gaulle*. (Weidenfeld & Nicolson, London 1960; Simon & Schuster, New York, 1960.)

The West meant the democracies: Great Britain, under Churchill, and America, led by Roosevelt. On June 15th, 1940, Churchill had proposed to me a generous plan—a Franco-British union, which I was the only member of my government to accept; and, on the day after the armistice with Germany which, despite a solemn pledge, removed the French fleet from the Allied camp, it was Churchill who promised France to continue the war until the day she should be restored 'to her grandeur and dignity', and who kept his word. Roosevelt, even before the entry of his country into the war, had sent us arms at my request. When he died de Gaulle made a moving funeral speech in his honour.[1]

The East meant Stalin's Russia, an ally of France who, on the eve of the war, had gone over to the enemy.

What was at the root of de Gaulle's policies? One fundamental thing: his hostility to the Americans and the British. We already knew that before, but now we have the documentation: Roosevelt's and Churchill's correspondence. How he exasperated Roosevelt! Churchill was unwilling to break with de Gaulle because he represented the French Resistance, but he had 'no confidence in de Gaulle's friendship for the Allies' and the sarcasm of his remarks about de Gaulle need not be quoted here. These were feelings, one guesses, that de Gaulle reciprocated a hundredfold. M. Corbin, who had been our Ambassador in London up to the armistice, who was summoned by de Gaulle after the war, has since told me that at their meeting 'all he talked to me about were his complaints against the English and the Americans . . .'

But by what right, having become a statesman, did he for this reason overturn France's traditional policy, the policy of solidarity with the two great democratic powers of Great Britain and the United States?— when in spite of the deplorable armistice, Churchill, alone and upright amid the tempest, had still promised France that his people would fight on until the day when France should be restored to her greatness and dignity!—and when this promise had indeed been kept at the cost of such great perils—when the American and British landing in Normandy had made them the liberators of France! Having become the head of his nation, it would have been seemly for de Gaulle to say, with Louis XII, 'The King of France does not exact vengeance for the wrongs committed upon the Duke of Orleans.' But he did otherwise.

Once back in London, he worked to keep the Americans and British out of the European continent.

[1] I feel bound to add that on visiting de Gaulle on my return from exile, to my question, 'And Roosevelt? What do you think of him?' He replied: 'Very bad.'

11

When we come to describe his military policy, closely modelled as it should be on his foreign policy, we shall see how, in 1950, after the Soviet annexation of Czechoslovakia, he declared that it was up to France to organise the defence of Europe. As for the Americans, let them confine their attentions to the Pacific, and the British to the Far East! This when America, playing the part of *leader* of the free world, was making a great effort to create an 'Atlantic defence force'.

Although he admitted at one time or another the need for the protection of the American nuclear missiles, at the same time he cast doubts on their willingness to defend us.

Western Europe as arbitrator between the USSR and the United States.

To the three solutions already mentioned, de Gaulle, in the same passage of his *Memoirs*, added a fourth—the most sensational—'To group, from the political, economic and strategic points of view, the States which border on the Rhine, the Alps and the Pyrenees'. In other words the six countries of the present-day Common Market, plus Franco's Spain. Great Britain and the United States, France's allies, are excluded. They are replaced by our two former enemies, Germany and Italy.

With what aim in mind? 'To make this organisation one of the three great world powers', the other two being Russia, whose forces had played the major part in the destruction of the German army, and America, who had staged the Normandy landing!

What an illusion! Before acquiring the atomic bomb, Russia had a crushing superiority in divisions of the conventional type, inspired by the flush of victory. For, in contrast to the democracies, Russia was careful not to disarm after the war. And nobody could tell if she would disarm in the future.

In order to realise de Gaulle's plan, in the face of the powerful and highly organised Russia and America, the countries of Western Europe had to be united. But de Gaulle has consistently refused this very union. How then could these independent morsels of Europe be persuaded to produce a collective military effort great enough to put Europe on the same footing as the two giants, Russia and America?

But let us read the conclusion: ' . . . and if necessary, one day, to act as arbitrator between the two sides—the Soviet and the Anglo-Saxon'.

In plain words: an exhausted Germany whose people would reply 'without us' to any suggestion of putting on uniform again; a ravaged

France whose army was just being re-formed; Italy, Spain and the three Benelux countries—these formed the future arbitrator between the Soviet and the Anglo-Saxon sides!

All this was to take place, of course, without the United States, left to its own devices, and without Great Britain!

The effect would be to hand over to the Russians a ruined, dismembered and defeated Germany and to run the risk that in her plight she would agree to reunification at the price of becoming Russia's leading satellite.

What would then have become of France?

These were the contradictory solutions which, to our surprise, de Gaulle blazoned forth as his 'vast plan'. We shall see, however, that he was to persevere with his plans.

On July 9th, 1947, addressing the Anglo-American press in Paris, de Gaulle, who had retired from power eighteen months previously, spoke of 'recreating the old Europe and recreating it as a community . . . It is in this way, and in this way alone, that there could exist, beside the two great powers, the element of stability without which peace would be lost in advance.' Naturally it would be a Europe without Great Britain.

De Gaulle expanded several times on this theme, but without giving any precise details as to how Europe was to be 're-created'.

This stubborn demand for a Europe which, when capable of becoming a reality, he was to prevent from emerging, is one of the outstanding features of his foreign policy.

Europe from the Atlantic to the Urals.

The fifth solution, 'Europe from the Atlantic to the Urals', was his first thought as soon as Paris had been liberated.

Another illusion! For as we can see today, the Soviet giant can only be counter-balanced by the American giant, Canada and the free countries of Europe, including Great Britain. A dialogue between Stalin and de Gaulle would have been like that of a wolf and a lamb. At the time de Gaulle considered that it would be easy for the Allies to obtain freedom for the satellites—a hope which I imagine must have quickly been dispelled. During my first conversation with Mr Khruschev in 1958, when I asked him about the reunification of Germany, he replied forcefully: 'Never!'

Henceforward, de Gaulle was alternately to champion 'Europe the third force' and 'Europe from the Atlantic to the Urals'. These day-dreams of a young general remind me of that picture of the sleeping Saint-Cyr cadet, dreaming at the foot of the standards.

And now I am bound to resort to quotations, for these extracts are evidence in the case I intend to prove. I shall present them in chrono-logical order to show that de Gaulle's reasoning has never developed.

On July 29th, 1946, six months after resigning from power, de Gaulle declared: 'What, then, can restore stability, if not the old world between two new worlds?' He then spoke of Europe in the guise of a fanatical European: '*What weight the nations situated in western Europe could bring to bear if they succeeded in combining their policies in spite,of age-old disagreements!*'[1]

Here we have the same mistake in evaluating the comparative strengths of the three blocs!

On June 29th, 1947, at Lille, he depicted Western Europe as capable of 'checking any possible bid for supremacy'[2] and of establishing between the two rival giants the 'element of stability indispensable to peace'.

Completely unrealistic! Had it not been for the Americans, the Russians, who in the following year were to seize Czechoslovakia, might have advanced as far as Brest! So much for Europe as the arbitrator between the two rival power blocs.

On March 16th, 1950, at the Palais d'Orsay, de Gaulle declared: 'I am convinced that if France, on her feet again and with proper leader-ship, took the initiative of calling upon Europe to unite . . . the whole European atmosphere from the Atlantic to the Urals would be changed, and even the men in power on the other side of the Iron Curtain would feel the consequences.'

Yet as soon as the 'leadership' of France was in his hands he antago-nised all his partners in the Common Market by refusing to create a united Europe!

On November 12th, 1953, at the Hotel Continental, de Gaulle re-called that 'Europe to the Urals' was an old ideal of his: 'I do not forget that Europe extends from Gibraltar to the Urals and, whatever my opinion of certain regimes, I have been in Moscow as well as in London and Brussels, and I have established relations with both Madrid and Ankara. In my opinion anyone who sincerely wishes it could take part in a united Europe.'

Even Soviet Russia herself, then at the height of the cold war with the West!

---

[1] My italics.
[2] This would apply as much to Anglo-Saxon as to Russian supremacy.

On April 7th, 1954, he said in Paris: 'I have, in fact, always wanted a united Europe to evolve from the disasters of the war. But I see Europe as she is. I see her stretching from Gibraltar to the Urals, from Spitzbergen to Sicily.'

And in an allusion to America, he wanted a Europe 'called upon to form a unique and tightly-knit organisation and not split into separate elements according to a convenient partitioning of the New World pattern.' Has this united Europe in fact come to pass? Alas, no. For alone, against the wishes of all our partners in the Common Market, de Gaulle was to oppose it when he came to power.

On April 25th, 1960, before the United States Congress, assembled in his honour, he declared: 'It is only by the organisation of a united Western Europe, opposed to the bloc created by the Russians, that a balance between the two zones, comparable in numbers and resources, can be achieved from the Atlantic to the Urals.' The gigantic military effort which Europe would have to make, the need for integration to this end—all this in fact could come about by 'the organisation of a united Western Europe'. But we shall find de Gaulle refusing to go further than 'simple cooperation', while repeating the need for European integration in his subsequent speeches.

And what of the United States? She would have the modest role of assistant to the old continent which, together with America, would 'be able at its leisure to help in the development of the deprived masses of Asia and Africa'. Uncle Sam, therefore, appears in the guise of an elderly military pensioner devoted to works of charity.

At that time, however, the members of Congress applauded de Gaulle.

In reality the supremacy of the Russians over Western Europe, after the departure of the US army, would either lead to the subjection of Western Europe or to a war from which America could not stand aside.

On March 13th, 1963, former Secretary of State Dean Acheson, President Kennedy's diplomatic adviser, speaking at Berkeley, California, was in no mood for applause. He declared: 'We would be assigned to defend Europe against the inevitable consequences of his [de Gaulle's] policy—domination by the Soviet Union—while being excluded from any part or influence in establishing in Western Europe what General Washington called "a respectable defensive posture". Our task under those circumstances would require the mutual incineration of the Soviet Union and the United States. It is difficult to conceive of any government in this country undertaking so unpromising a commitment.'

15

One can understand Dean Acheson! The prerequisite of the de Gaulle system would have been a united Western Europe in possession of the deterrent and imposing upon itself very heavy sacrifices for its defence. De Gaulle never alludes to these conditions.

On May 31st, 1960, a month after his speech to the American Congress, de Gaulle called for 'the organisation of a Western group [European] at least equivalent to that which exists in the East',[1] to 'establish the European entente between the Atlantic and the Urals'.

In token of this we shall see him torpedo the modest Fouchet Plan, which merely envisaged occasional talks between heads of states or between European governments, with the vague hope of future integration. According to him Europe must remain a body without a head!

But in August, 1961, the Berlin wall cut the city in two! Two months later, on October 2nd, 1961, de Gaulle, in a television interview spoke once more of 'a balanced Europe from the Atlantic to the Urals, as soon as totalitarian imperialism halts its ambitious designs there'. In fact, we were in the middle of a cold war.

On May 15th, 1962, when the cold war was at its height, he expressed this wish: 'If in Western Europe a firm, prosperous and attractive organisation can be created, then the possibilities of a European balance with the Eastern states and the prospects of a *genuinely European cooperation* will reappear, particularly if at the same time the totalitarian regime ceases to poison the springs.'

'Genuinely European!' The main idea was still to exclude the Anglo-Saxons. And by then the Russians already possessed an impressive nuclear arsenal.

On June 17th, 1962, he exclaimed: 'This great Europe [from the Atlantic to the Urals] with the assistance of the New World, which is her offspring, could then solve the problem of the misery of the 2,000 million inhabitants of the under-developed countries.' The 'assistance' therefore was still confined to works of charity!

On September 4th, 1962, at Bonn, he spoke once more of 'from the Atlantic to the Urals', on the express condition that a flourishing and powerful European community exists in the West; in other words essentially a Franco-German policy—a formula calculated to create anger and disquiet among the other members of the Common Market.

He is confident that, in the West at least, he will be the leader, thanks to his striking force. But he forgets what would happen in the event of a nuclear duel between France and Russia!

[1] The satellite countries.

The Germans however, being realists, know perfectly well that Soviet missiles cannot be stopped by this kind of rhetoric. Their attitude towards the United States is also one of the numerous points of disagreement, as we shall see, between them and de Gaulle. They want the Americans in Europe because the security of us all depends on their presence.

On December 11th, 1962, in his message to the National Assembly which had just been elected, de Gaulle acknowledged that the Atlantic alliance was indispensable for the defence of the free world and demanded the French striking force. But we shall see how he then opposed any integration of the national forces within NATO.

On December 31st, 1962, in a television address, he favoured the union of Western Europe 'to establish a balance with the United States'. This union would be *'ready in the future* to welcome a Great Britain which could and would join it, *finally and without reservations'*.[1]

This union, he said, would subsequently tend to organise Europe from the Atlantic to the Urals, when the day 'the great easing of tension' between East and West came. Such a Europe, with its top-level discussions, according to his formula, would be on an equal footing with the United States! As far as Great Britain was concerned, a fortnight later he vetoed her entry into the Common Market. This was the end of Europe from the Atlantic to the Urals.

On January 29th, 1963, Mr Vinogradov, the Soviet Ambassador, was received at the Élysée Palace. On February 5th, the Soviet Ambassador issued a communiqué to the press making it clear that 'contrary to information published by the French press, the meeting of January 29th had been arranged on the initiative of the President of the Republic and not of the Soviet Embassy'. According to René Courtin[2], de Gaulle had asked for this interview to disclose to the ambassador his great plan of 'the Atlantic to the Urals', as seems probable from the statement made by Maurice Couve de Murville, our Minister for Foreign Affairs, before the Senate Commission for Foreign Affairs on February 14th, 1963. This statement seems in fact to announce the setback of de Gaulle's efforts: 'For the moment it can be stated that the USSR does not seek an agreement with the Europe of the Six, and is not inclined to conduct any discussions other than with the United States.'[3]

Did this affront, implicit in Mr Vinogradov's communiqué, signify,

[1] My italics.
[2] *L'Europe de l'Atlantique à l'Oural*, a remarkable book from which several of the above quotations have been taken.
[3] *Le Monde*, February 15th, 1963.

as has been said, Moscow's definite rejection of 'Europe from the Atlantic to the Urals'? The Russians whom I questioned replied: 'De Gaulle has never clearly stated what he means by "Europe from the Atlantic to the Urals" for the very good reason that he knows it to be impossible.' This was the death-blow to the great plan.

In July, 1963, the heavyweight boxer Kruschev came to an agreement with the heavyweight Kennedy, whose power he rightly respected. He ignored the French lightweight. But one shudders to think of the danger that Europe, and as a result France, would have run had Stalin or Khruschev said to de Gaulle: 'I recognise you as the head of Western Europe. I agree to deal with you. Because of my generals I cannot immediately free the satellites which form our bulwark against Europe, who attacked and invaded us in 1813 and in 1941, but I will tell you the conditions under which I could accept your plan.'

What a danger this would have posed, in a country like France, where so many discontented electors vote Communist. Either with or without direct Russian intervention, what kind of status would France have been bound to accept?

The end of a dangerous dream.

When the dream in which America would be excluded from the United States of Europe ended, de Gaulle was lead to declare in September, 1963, on his tour of South-eastern France, that he did not wish to be protected by the Americans—a bitter reaction on seeing an unrealisable ambition vanish into thin air and the result of the Russian rebuff.

He was to go even further, taking the offensive by intervening in Vietnam, at a time when the Americans found themselves in a most difficult situation as a result of having taken over France's responsibilities after their defeat at Dien Bien Phu. He strengthened the Communists in Vietnam by recognising Mao Tse Tung's China, without consultation beforehand with our American allies, and then pronounced his intention to visit South America, another trouble spot.

All this despite the fact that the presence of United States troops in Europe guarantees our safety. He has never forgiven them for being there with their power and prestige.

The fact is that La Rochefoucauld was right when he spoke of great men and their faults.

CHAPTER 2 *Barring the way to European unity*

My attitude towards Europe.

IT WOULD BE DIFFICULT TO IMAGINE MORE DIAMETRICALLY OPPOSED stands than those taken by de Gaulle and me on the subject of Europe.

After the victory of 1918, realising that France had lost all her great allies, I came to the conclusion that she would have to fight again one day, at odds of two to one, if she allowed Germany to rearm. It was therefore absolutely essential to divest Germany of any *possibility* of revenge. That is why in 1924 I demanded that our defensive army should be replaced by an efficient offensive force, which by lightning action would prevent Germany from rearming, in defiance of the Versailles Treaty. This was what I called the 'treaty army'[1].

My advice was not followed. It was useless my predicting that if we retained our defensive army we should see the German army 'hold out a hand to the Red Army over the corpse of Poland, France being invaded once more, our factories destroyed and our graveyards desecrated'. These predictions impressed no one. But sixteen years later they came true.

Incidentally, I thought it necessary to progress beyond the nationalist sentiments which the war had inflamed, and to create the basis of a future Europe by an economic *entente* with Germany, which would have solved the problem of reparations. It was because Poincaré refused to take advantage of the 'Victory of the Ruhr'[2] to realise this *entente*, that I

[1] 'Do we possess the army we need or the army which we are used to?' (*Revue hebdomadaire,* July 5th, 1924.)
[2] In January, 1923, President Poincaré sent French troops to occupy the Ruhr to enforce payments of reparation by Germany. In August, 1925, after the Dawes plan was signed, France was persuaded to withdraw her troops.

came into conflict with him, as I have related in the first volume of my *Memoirs*[1].

After World War II, on return from captivity, I went to see my friend Duff Cooper[2], at that time British Ambassador in Paris. He asked me what conclusions I had drawn from my reflections during 56 months in prison. I replied: 'That your country and mine are too small to live in isolation in the modern world.' He merely shrugged his shoulders. Since then I have never ceased to fight for Europe.

In 1948, at the Hague European Congress convened by Winston Churchill, it was suggested that we should create a Consultative Assembly of the Council of Europe. It would be composed of representatives of France, Great Britain, Belgium, the Netherlands and Luxembourg, who would eventually be joined by those of Germany and Italy. All of them would be appointed by their respective Parliaments. I caused a minor scandal by voting for an amendment, together with Édouard Bonnefous and René Courtin, according to which the members of the Assembly should be elected by universal suffrage. I received eight votes out of five hundred. During my whole career this is the vote of which I am proudest; for nine years later the Treaty of Rome would provide for this mode of election, and today all the 'Europeans' demand it.

Since then, both at the Council of Europe in Strasbourg and in the French National Assembly, both at home and abroad[3], I have never ceased fighting for the European ideal. M. Marjolin, Vice-President of the Commission for the European Community, had the same ideal in mind when he described the world of 1973, more or less in the following terms: if the Europe we desired were created, we could expect three great world powers—Europe with 280 million inhabitants, Russia with 250 million and the United States with 200 million. Such a unified Europe would be a continent encouraging the aspirations of young people who could travel freely without a passport, visa or customs inspection, using a common currency. Anyone would be able to buy and sell as he pleased, and would have the opportunity to try his luck in any chosen field and to settle anywhere under conditions of absolute equality.

Today only the three great powers are mentioned. On several occasions at Strasbourg I tried to encourage my British friends to take a

[1] *Memoirs* (Flammarion, Paris).
[2] British Minister of Information during the Second World War.
[3] I made two lecture tours in the United States on this subject, one with Lord Layton, who was at that time Vice-President of the Consultative Assembly of the Council of Europe.

bolder stand on the problem of Europe. I said to them one day: 'I understand your policy. You tell us: build your European house. If all goes well we will take the flat you will certainly have reserved for us. If the house collapses about your ears we shall attend your funeral with the greatest sympathy.'

In power, Churchill abandoned the idea of the European army, which he had initiated together with André Philip and myself, and which had been voted by the Strasbourg Assembly. This led to the failure of the European Defence Community.

With regard to foreign affairs, I myself have always favoured France's traditional policy, that of a close union with the United States and Great Britain. In my opinion the democracies form one large family inspired by a common ideal. I have a very vivid recollection of the reaction to my appeal in favour of a union of the democracies against the threat of the Italian and German dictators, at a Congress of the American Bar Association, on October 14th 1932, during the worst period of the economic crisis and in spite of unpaid war debts. As I left the audience gave me a standing ovation.

De Gaulle and the German problem.

As a soldier between the two wars de Gaulle could take no official stand. After the Second World War his first thought was the dismemberment of Germany. On February 24th, 1944, he wrote a letter to his Minister for Foreign Affairs, René Massigli, in which he envisaged the separation of the Rhineland and Germany. 'No more centralised-Reich!' he declared. 'In my opinion,' he wrote in his *Memoirs* 'this was the first condition for preventing Germany from reverting to her evil ways'[1].

De Gaulle was in favour of a confederation, but forseeing that a German confederation would gradually tend to become a highly centralised state, he urged that the left bank of the Rhine should be converted into a bulwark for France, Belgium and Holland, and even Great Britain.

At the end of 1949 he was still demanding a confederation of the German states, but the aggressive attitude of the USSR forced the Americans and the British to put Germany back on her feet again. On September 7th, 1949, the Federal German Republic was proclaimed. Henceforward, there was no further question of dismembering Germany.

[1] *Salvation.*

21

De Gaulle concurred, reluctantly abandoning his idea of a confederation of German states.

On March 16th, 1950, at the Palais d'Orsay, it seemed to some that he was dreaming of reviving the empire of Charlemagne, along modern lines. Even in 1963 at the Elysée, when he embraced Chancellor Adenauer after the signing of the Franco-German Treaty, some of our partners in the Common Market suspected that he had not altogether forgotten his dream of 1949. This gave rise to a fear that in future the affairs of Europe would be settled over their heads.

De Gaulle's 'Federation' and 'Confederation'.

Let us now examine de Gaulle's ideas, before his return to power in 1958, concerning the creation of a united Europe. On several occasions he had insisted that it was úp to France to create Europe and to lead it.

On April 20th, 1943, he declared: 'In a Europe which will now resume its progress at the clear, swift pace dictated by modern technology . . . the French sense *what an important part French genius* will be called upon to play.'[1]

On March 7th, 1948, he said at Compiègne: 'In a group whose arteries are the North Sea, the Rhine, and the Mediterranean, the duty and privilege of being the *centre and the key* must devolve upon France.'

On February 11th, 1950, he declared at the Vélodrome d'Hiver: 'Europe will not materialise unless France assumes the leadership.' And for the benefit of the leaders of that period he added: 'I mean a France on her feet and without borders.' No comment.

On July 10th, 1950, he stated to the United Press: 'As soon as France has a policy, she must take another road and carry the continent with her.' Excellent! For in fact here and only here on the international political plane can France be 'in the forefront'.

Let us now see what kind of administrative framework he advocates. He has put forward various solutions, one after the other. On April 21st, 1944, at his press conference, he took a grandiose view: 'We feel it desirable, particularly from the economic point of view, that a *kind of group* should be created in Western Europe, the arteries of which might be the Channel, the Mediterranean and the Rhine. This would seem to provide an element of European organisation, *within the world organisation*, which would present certain advantages for everyone, and in

[1] The italics here and in the following de Gaulle quotations are mine.

particular for the interested states. *I believe that we are living in a period of concentration.*'

At a press conference of October 12th, 1945, de Gaulle looked beyond Europe. He made statements which today he would consider too rash: 'The world must be organised. *A Western organisation could do no harm to the European organisation—on the contrary. And a European organisation could do* no harm to a world organisation.'

Since then he has gone into reverse . . .

On July 6th, 1952, de Gaulle said at the closing session of the National Council of the RPF[1] 'The immense edifice we have to build is today called Europe. There will be no Europe unless it is created *by the nations and with their active participation in it.*'

On November 12th, 1953, at a press conference in Paris, de Gaulle produced another formula: 'France conceives such an organisation as *an association of nations*, each bringing to the common task its personality and value, while preserving, of course, its individual character and guise.'

On June 25th, 1950, at the National Assizes of the RPF he proclaimed: 'A solemn referendum of all free Europeans must give birth to the *Federation*, define its scope, and create its institutions.'

Unfortunately the Germans, disgusted with dictatorship, whose favourite weapon is the referendum, have banned it from their constitution.

On July 10th, 1950, de Gaulle declared to the United Press: 'On the basis of this agreement between France and Germany . . . we must progress towards an *effective European Federation* between those who wish to be members of it, and leaving outside those who do not wish to join.'

On June 22nd, 1951, at a press conference at the Palais d'Orsay: 'We are in favour of a *European Federation*, in other words of an agreement which links the states of Europe who are in favour of it, *in a practical manner*, in practical projects—particularly in the fields of economics, defence and culture.'

It is worth remarking that the Atlantic Treaty had already linked the United States and the countries of Western Europe in the field of common defence.

The *Dictionnaire Larousse* gives the following definition of confederation: 'A union of States subject to a general authority whilst retaining their individual forms of government.' For example, the Swiss Confederation.

---

[1] Rassemblement du Peuple Français, his party at that time.

Switzerland in fact would be an admirable model for Europe. She resembles a miniature Europe composed of three nations speaking different languages. Yet they speak neither Volapuk nor Esperanto. The educated classes, in addition to their own, learn one or both of the other languages.

Let us now take a look at history so as to clarify our ideas.

Napoleon I dissolved the Holy Roman Empire and created a confederation out of the territories of sixteen independent German princes, who recognised the French Emperor as their protector.

After the fall of Napoleon a confederation was created which included, in addition to the sovereigns of the German states, the Emperor of Austria, who became their legal president. A Diet composed of plenipotentiaries of these sovereigns sat at Frankfurt. It was empowered to take decisions on matters of common interest. Its weakness was inadequate authority; but nevertheless it did possess some practical authority.

After the Austro-Prussian War of 1866, Austria and the southern states were excluded from the confederation, which was now dominated by Prussia and had as its president the King of Prussia, and as its chancellor Bismarck.

After the German victory of 1871 over France, the confederation became the German Empire. This was merely a change of names.

The essence of a confederation is, as we know, to be vested with an authority superior to that of its members, in so far as concerns their common interests.

Here are seven speeches from press conferences in which de Gaulle has demanded a Confederation of Europe:

1. The closing speech to the RPF, Saint-Mandé, November 4th, 1951: 'When I was in power immediately after the victory I did my best to get France to take the first steps in this direction on her own initiative. Yes, I wanted us to rise above history and accept Germany into a *Federated Europe*, conditional upon her accepting ties and obligations which would prevent her from reverting to her old habits.'

2. The closing speech at the National Assizes of the RPF, Nancy, November 25th, 1951: 'It is only within the framework, the ties and obligations of the confederated Europe which we desire, that the various armies of the Continent, including that of Germany, could in favourable conditions be combined without being merged.'

3. Press conference at the Palais d'Orsay, December 21st, 1951: 'We could do much better. We could create the *Confederation of Europe* in which each nation, including Germany, would have its forces, on

certain conditions and according to precise and categorical obligations.'
And he adds this crucial phrase: ' . . . a confederation of states constituting *inter se a common confederal power to which each delegates a part of its sovereignty, in particular in the fields of economy, defence and culture.*'

An excellent definition! What are we asking for today? What have we always asked? Just this.

But alas de Gaulle, on his return to power in 1958, was no longer in favour of it and offered our partners only the shame of a 'Europe of individual countries', deprived of the supranational power they desired —a Europe rather like a man without a head.

4. Speech at the Vélodrome d'Hiver, February 23rd, 1952: 'In *handing back the securities we hold in Germany* we would have to exchange them for the *organisation of Europe into a genuine confederation.*'

5. Speech of May 1st, 1952: 'A United Europe? Of course! *But it would have to be a genuine confederation.*'

6. On October 8th, 1952, he condensed into a single phrase an attack on the Schuman Plan and the need to create a confederation: 'We must see that Europe, the major hope of the world, is established not as an imbroglio of "pools" but as a confederation of states.'

7. And on October 12th, 1952, he repeated: 'We must accept the realities as they are, in other words *national*, and unite the nations in a confederation, France playing a prominent role thanks, chiefly, to the French Union.'

What did de Gaulle do as soon as he was faced with realities? He vainly opposed the Schuman Plan to create the Coal and Steel Community. He contributed largely to the defeat of the plan for the European Defence Community. He caused his followers to vote against the ratification of the Rome Treaty in Parliament, the Rome Treaty which created the European Economic Community—the Common Market.

As for his fine schemes for federation and confederation, they evaporated. Finally the mountain gave birth to a mouse: occasional meetings of heads of state or of governments, in which everyone possessed the right of veto . . .

De Gaulle opposes the Schuman Plan.

On the death of Robert Schuman, the Pope, President Kennedy and all the European statesmen expressed their admiration and respect for this tall, slender, modest man. He was so calm, so discreet, one of the great men in a period which produced so few.

In 1919 we both joined the Chamber of the National Bloc[1], and in my government during the war he accepted responsibility for the refugees.

In 1949 he negotiated and signed the Atlantic pact which saved Western Europe after the Communist coup in Czechoslovakia.

It was through Europe that Robert Schuman became a great Frenchman. His crowning glory was to have laid the foundation stone of Europe at the suggestion of Jean Monnet. His famous declaration of May 9th, 1950, announced the Schuman Plan, the main aim of which, according to him, 'was to make a new war between France and Germany impossible'. It was a question of creating a Coal and Steel Community, known as the ECSC, by placing under a European authority the two products which provide the basis of a nation's arms industry. A supranational power was created: the Coal and Steel Authority, composed of members from the six countries which created this community. Thanks to Robert Schuman, France had the honour of having taken the initiative —an action of capital importance recorded to our credit by all nations.

One man however, opposed Schuman—a famous man whose nationalism forbids his crossing the threshold of Europe because he refuses Europe the authority which it merits, which *in its sphere of action* supersedes that of the governments of the states composing it. De Gaulle fought the Schuman Plan with a weapon which its author least deserved: contempt. It was through ridicule that he tried to destroy this first European organisation. Attacking Schuman on his home ground before the mayors and municipal councillors of the Moselle, he said: 'We are being offered a hotchpotch of coal and steel.'

On December 21st, 1951, he went so far as to say that the coal and steel plan and the plan for creating a European army were only tiresome schemes 'which ran the risk of harming the idea of Europe'. Robert Schuman harming Europe!

Because the officials of ECSC were European-minded, de Gaulle accused them of forming a 'kind of synarchy'. He refused to see that the European spirit could serve France by serving Europe.

On October 6th he scoffed at the 'imbroglio of pools'. A month later at the Vélodrome d'Hiver, he declared: 'The Franco-German merger into a series of economic and military entities, born of obscure deliberations and governed by technocrats, is nothing but a scheme devised by tight-rope walkers.'

---

[1] Dominated by conservative ex-servicemen, it cut across the Radicals but excluded the Socialists.

The technocrats he so much despised were those high officials of the Coal and Steel Authority, later to become the Commission of the Common Market at Brussels, whose success is now universally acknowledged, and who were to save Europe and French agriculture in their discussions on December 23rd, 1963.

De Gaulle fought the Schuman Plan in Parliament with his partisans. In the Assembly one of the heads of the RPF, whose career has certainly not suffered by this intervention, announced that the result of the Schuman Plan for France would be 'a veritable catastrophe'.

One trembles to think what would have happened had de Gaulle possessed in the Assembly the unconditional majority[1] he enjoys today. The Schuman Plan would have been torn to shreds.

But the Assembly, composed largely of representatives of the 'old parties', as de Gaulle calls them, ratified the Schuman Plan on December 13th, 1951, by 377 votes to 236 votes—the opposition comprising Gaullists, Communists and extreme Right Wingers.

In the Senate, Michel Debré, de Gaulle's future premier and the most reliable representative of Gaullist thought, fought the Schuman Plan by asking: 'Who would not be disturbed by the trends of German youth?' and asserting that although one day it would be necessary to forget, it was dangerous to do so at the moment. 'The Coal and Steel Community,' he concluded, 'is a policy which is not lacking in grandeur. Unfortunately it is a false idea.'

This 'false idea' was the idea of a Franco-German reconciliation, the foundation stone of Europe. The Coal and Steel Community—the Schuman Plan—was ratified in the Senate by 184 votes to 90, opposed in the main by Gaullists, Communists and members of the extreme Right. De Gaulle continued his campaign.

On March 10th, 1952, at his press conference, he declared that the Coal and Steel Community was only a 'blind'. On October 8th, 1952, he launched a further attack at a press conference: 'We must continue to arrange for Europe to be established . . . not as an imbroglio of "pools" but as a confederation of states.' Alas, he did not want a confederation of states either.

It is understandable that, threatened with the torpedoing of his European policy on de Gaulle's return to power, Robert Schuman should have supported all the motions of censure during his remaining years in the Parliament. On account of Algeria and my friendship with de Gaulle I abstained until the day he violated his own Constitution.

[1] A majority in force since the National Assembly election of November, 1962.

Europe? Volapuk or Esperanto!

On November 12th, 1952, forgetting that the Bretons and the Flemings have never ceased to love Brittany and Flanders because they became French, and that the French would no more cease to love France if they became Europeans, de Gaulle, forgetting federation and confederation, accused the champions of Europe of trying to create stateless persons: 'One is not a European if one is a man without a country. Chateaubriand, Goethe, Byron and Tolstoy would have been worth nothing at all in Volapuk or Esperanto.'

These are arguments that he repeated ten years later at his press conference of May 15th, 1962, and which have recently lost him Pfimlin and his friends of the MRP[1] in the Pompidou government. De Gaulle calls supranational Europe 'that monster, that robot', and here we get down to bedrock.

A century earlier Victor Hugo said: 'The nations must not be destroyed, but brought into a common fold, like sisters around the hearth, each with her own personality and familiar face.' In brief, to form a single family. What a setback a century and a half later under de Gaulle!

1957. De Gaulle threatens to 'tear up' the Treaty of Rome which created the Common Market.

Then came the rebuff to the European Defence Community (EDC) caused by the opposition of de Gaulle and his friends, and by the division of the various parliamentary groups. This was de Gaulle's only success in all the battles he waged against Europe when he was in the opposition. Michel Debré sent a letter to leading personalities known to be favourable towards EDC in which he declared that the Treaty of Rome was infamous. He added: 'That it should have been signed is in itself highly improper.' Hence the violence with which the Gaullists fought it. Later we shall see de Gaulle bitterly oppose the integration of the national armies within NATO.

The pro-Europeans were determined to get their own back. They got it with the Treaty of Rome, which in 1957 created the Common Market. Once again, but in vain, de Gaulle tried to crush this European creation whose brilliant success, as we shall see, contributed largely to his own victory in the anti-constitutional referendum of October, 1962, and in the general elections of the following month.

[1] Mouvement Républicain Populaire.

In 1957 the National Assembly, the Gaullists, were reduced to less than a score. They chose as their spokesman Raymond Dronne, who has since left them. He announced on July 3rd, 1957, without beating about the bush: 'The Common Market would be a disaster for France.'

In the Council of the Republic (which once more became the Senate in 1958) on July 19th, 1957, Michel Debré gave a speech which took up nine pages of the official bulletin. He brought all his oratory gifts to bear in airing de Gaulle's and his own philosophy. It took the form of a full-scale offensive against the Common Market. He attacked its very principles: 'Opposition to the principle of national protectionism is a mistake,' he said. Yet this is the very soul of the Common Market! When it becomes fully effective the customs belt will encircle all the member nations. There will be no separating barrier between them.

As for the Commission of the European Economic Community, Debré complains that this body will always prevail over the individual governments. If the Commission did so prevail on December 23rd, 1963, it was by persuading the ministers concerned. In so doing it rescued French agriculture! Debré's arguments seem to date from the last century. Regarding Europe he does not talk, as de Gaulle does, about 'co-operation' between nations, but says: 'The very idea of European integration spells an end to French freedom of action,' and again: 'We can only recover by ourselves . . . We have nothing to expect from foreigners, apart from mutual friendship when we ourselves are strong enough to be accepted as friends by others.' Fortunately, this formula does not apply to us vis-a-vis NATO! And what about this for finality: 'The plans for integration [contained in the Treaty of Rome and very modest] which are proposed to you, mean the disappearance of our nation.'

This is Gaullist foreign policy plain and unvarnished.

Michel Debré was in no doubt that his condemnation of the Common Market, against which he had voted, would result in national prosperity and that people would feel that they owed this to de Gaulle. This would influence the latter in his decision to violate the Constitution and thus ensure the continuation of the policies which Debré had defended in the Senate!

We shall see all this in due course.

The Treaty of Rome was ratified in the National Assembly by 340 votes to 236 (opposed mainly by Communists, Gaullists, and members of the extreme Right) and in the Council of the Republic by 184 votes to 90. Here again, let us repeat, what a disaster it would have been for

Europe and for France had he enjoyed today's Gaullist majority in the whole of the Chamber!

The threat of Debré.

That same year, 1957, Michel Debré denounced the legality of the Rome Treaty and stated that were it to be ratified by Parliament it would, one of these days, by one means or another, have to be destroyed.[1]

Such a serious proclamation could not have been made without de Gaulle's authority. In fact, although on his return to power he was forced to give support to the Common Market, we shall see that he deliberately undermined NATO by refusing to create the essential political institutions which everyone expected. To complete the picture, let us add that at the same time he undermined his own Constitution, at first by his speeches and, when in power, by further speeches and by a decree. This last point will be the object of my study on the Constitution which will shortly be published.

December 24th, 1958. I plead with de Gaulle for Europe.

The day after de Gaulle's election to the presidency of the Republic I took advantage of an aggressive declaration against Europe and the Common Market, made by an important Gaullist deputy, to point out to de Gaulle the conflict that this attitude could arouse in the minds of most deputies. I advised him to take a definite stand in order to ease the task of Michel Debré, the future Prime Minister, whose own past attitude would place him in a delicate position were this problem to be raised on the day he was to appear before the Assembly.

On December 24th, 1958, seven days after the launching of the Schuman Plan, I wrote him a letter in which I referred particularly to this deputy's attitude: 'To scoff at "little Europe" is a failure to recognise that it would have as large a population as the United States, with the the most highly qualified manpower in the world at its disposal.

'To maintain that the Common Market is a new "continental blockade" is a failure to realise that the exports of Great Britain to the six countries of the Common Market which, incidentally, represent only 12% of her total exports, would in no way be prohibited.

'To condemn the policy of obtaining the help of other European countries to make imperative investments in Africa and Madagascar,

[1] Roger Massip De Gaulle et l'Europe.

30

is to ignore the fact that we shall have to invest a minimum of one hundred thousand million francs a year in Algeria, and that our industrialists in metropolitan France lag behind their competitors in this respect.

'To demand, in present-day circumstances, a revision of the Treaty of Rome, and to try to "delay the actual launching of the Common Market", would be to give our partners in the Common Market a tempting opportunity to drop us.

'To reject the intended Franco-German *tête-à-tête* is a failure to realise that harnessing Western Germany to the West is the only way of preventing a successor of Adenauer from one day accepting Russian gifts, which they have in plenty, in return for consenting to become satellite No. 1 — which would settle the fate of both Germany and France.

'This is doubtless what we should hear maintained and answered on the platform, at the risk of splitting the majority in two, if such a debate took place.

'A polemicist has on occasion become a statesman, and I sincerely hope that this will be the case with Michel Debré. But his past pronouncements would cause him great embarrassment in this debate.

'It is with this danger in mind that I suggest to you the idea of settling this question in your speech on December 31st, in terms explicit enough to enable your successor[1] to refer to it and thus avoid a debate on this issue.'

De Gaulle replied to me in a very friendly letter in which he said: 'I have not failed to note what you write on the subject of Europe. You know that in my opinion one can regard it and perhaps create it in two ways: integration on supranational lines or by the cooperation of states and nations. Personally I adhere to the second choice.'

The truth is that de Gaulle wants neither a federation nor a confederation. For since then de Gaulle has revealed that at no price does he want Europe to possess any of the regimes he called for when he was in opposition. He was perfectly well aware of the nature of a confederation, since he demanded it for Germany. Once he came to power he no longer admitted that there should be a European authority superior to his own, let alone a federation. To the word confederation he gives another meaning, a very strange one: no supranational power, but occasional talks between heads of states or governments, where no decision can be taken unanimously. This is de Gaulle's confederation today. The total

---

[1] Michel Debré was to succeed him as Premier, de Gaulle having been elected President of the Republic.

impotence of such a regime has been shown by the setback to the Franco-German conversations held in July, 1963, six months after the signing of the treaty between the two countries.

It is obvious that each head of state or government would arrive at these talks imbued with the arguments of his own country, bringing reports drawn up by his own governmental departments. At this juncture a single voice against a proposal by one of the members would be enough to capsize it. And the secretariat of this so-called confederation would be composed of officials who were not 'Europeans' but *directly responsible to their own governments*. This is a fundamental error of conception. It is the reverse of the position held by the members of the Common Market Commission in Brussels. The members of this commission are not there to defend national interests, but attend as Europeans, whose duty is to defend the interests of Europe, which is the best method of protecting the interests of their own country. We know what authority this commission has acquired.

De Gaulle's confederation is an organisation of impotence.

July 30*th*, 1960. *Secret disagreement between de Gaulle and Adenauer at Rambouillet.*

Within the Common Market, negotiations were speeded up. The industrialists were equipped for the struggle. Industrial combines came into operation. The revolution caused by the Common Market among French industrialists has been summed up as follows by M. Georges Villiers, President of the Patronat[1]. 'Instead of being preoccupied with protecting themselves against foreign competition in their own market, our industrialists have substituted a determination to penetrate foreign markets. From the defensive they have gone over to the offensive.'

This is a renaissance in the economic field comparable with that which took place four centuries ago in the sphere of arts and letters. All the members of the Common Market are thereby enriched.

But de Gaulle will not admit that this success could be due to an authority placed above that of the individual countries. Leading officials of the Common Market appear to him to be stateless persons. He objects that the 'stateless men' of Brussels are considering sending ambassadors to their governments. This is too much for de Gaulle!

Moreover, he cannot tolerate the important part played by the Americans in the defence of Europe.

[1] Conseil National du Patronat français—Association of French employers.

These were the ideas which obsessed him when he decided upon the meeting between Adenauer and himself which took place in July, 1960.

Two years before, at Colombey-les-deux-Églises, he laid on all his charm for Adenauer and completely won him over. He was discreet on the subject of Europe. He intended to reap the profit from this on July 30–31, 1960, when he received the Chancellor in the Louis xv panelled rooms at the Château de Rambouillet. His firm resolve was to involve Adenauer in his fight against the Brussels technocrats and the American military minds.

The conversations lasted five hours, spread over those two days.

From the very start Adenauer found the President less of a good European than two years previously. Gradually, as de Gaulle mounted his offensives, the Chancellor's anxiety increased. His host went so far as to say that NATO must be reformed and that if he received no satisfaction he would leave it within three months.

Adenauer, who knew that without NATO Europe would suffer the fate of Czechoslovakia, was startled.

In temperate terms he pointed out that it was essential:
1. Not to give Soviet Russia the impression that the free world was divided.
2. To realise that without the aid of America, Europe would be lost.

These, he told de Gaulle, were the fundamental principles of European policy.

The Chancellor added that it was quite possible that NATO, which was only ten years old, might be in need of reforms, but it would be unwise to make public such plans at the present time, particularly now that the American electoral campaign was in full swing. It was more important to obtain American assurances concerning the use of tactical nuclear weapons upon which their common security depended.

With regard to the Common Market, he had discussed de Gaulle's grievances with Herr Hallstein, President of the Commission, who had replied that there was a choice of two policies: to consolidate the results already achieved or to speed up development. He had advised him to adopt the first solution. As to whether the Brussels Commission had really exceeded its powers, as de Gaulle maintained, he would make enquiries.

These wise and conciliatory words gave little satisfaction to the French President. No communiqué was issued to the press after these two-day conversations. Before leaving Rambouillet, Adenauer stressed to de Gaulle the potential danger of publishing the views which the latter had just expressed, and he confirmed this in a letter on his return to Bonn.

Was de Gaulle disappointed? Whatever his feelings he continued his offensive against the other members of the Common Market, taking a month to reply to Adenauer's letter. He had every confidence in himself, in his prestige and in his star.

German and French opinion after Rambouillet.

The German press got wind of the Rambouillet conversations and expressed its opposition to de Gaulle's ideas: 'No flirtation with the third force!' was the headline of the *Kölnische Rundschau* of August 2nd.

'Safeguard the Brussels institutions', said the *Neue Presse*.

'Nothing can replace the American alliance', asserted the *Frankfurter Allgemeine Zeitung*.

'To isolate London would spell the end of all European policy. There is already mention of a Paris-Bonn axis, which recalls a most unfortunate precedent', wrote the *Deutsche Zeitung*.

A very different light filtered through on the French side.

Beneath the headlines: 'Political Cooperation in Europe', *Le Monde* of August 3rd maintained that Rambouillet had ended with the Bonn government abandoning all solutions based on the principle of supra-nationalism, and that Adenauer was in agreement with de Gaulle on the question of occasional meetings between the heads of states or governments of the six countries of the Common Market.

Bonn reassures London.

London was afraid that an attempt had been made at Rambouillet to isolate Great Britain. The German ambassador in London, therefore, declared to the Press: 'It is not without significance that the forthcoming meeting of Macmillan and Adenauer was announced when the Chancellor was in France. This proves that the conversations at Rambouillet were not of an exclusive nature, and that anything which could harm future cooperation between England and the Six has been avoided. The forthcoming conversations at Bonn (Macmillan-Adenauer) must be envisaged as forming part of the Western effort to fill the void caused by the setback to the summit conference.'[1]

[1] A setback due to Khruschev's violent reaction towards the American spy-planes over Russian territory.

In the British view, Adenauer had been won over to the idea of re-shaping the form of political cooperation within the Atlantic alliance.

De Gaulle receives . . .

On August 31st, de Gaulle received the Dutch Prime Minister and Foreign Minister.

On September 3rd and 4th he received Signor Fanfani, the Italian President of the Council, and his Foreign Minister.

In the course of these visits he outlined the ideas which Adenauer had found dangerous or ill-timed, and which he had begged de Gaulle not to circulate.

September 5th, 1960. De Gaulle attacks Europe and NATO.

On September 5th, de Gaulle made a public attack during a press conference on the ideas of the 'Europeans': 'To imagine that one can build something effective for action which will be approved by the nations, outside or over the heads of the states themselves, is a chimera.' France's five partners in the Common Market thought otherwise.

Then came the offensive against NATO which had to be overhauled. De Gaulle no longer believed in integration. Had he ever believed in it? He demanded a revision of the treaties[1] on this point, but gave no specifications. He also attacked the technocrats to whom the success of the Common Market was due.

European reaction.

The German press reproached de Gaulle for having 'deceived his audience regarding the real jurisdiction of the communities', for 'remaining silent on the progress achieved as a result of European integration', and finally of 'endangering the balance achieved with so much effort within the heart of Europe'.

The *General Anzeiger* declared that what de Gaulle had said was a condemnation of everything which Dr Adenauer held sacred. It recalled that for ten years the latter had fought relentlessly for the integrity of Europe, that he had been the driving force which had launched the institutions of 'little Europe'. Now, it went on, de Gaulle indignantly rejected all these organisations. In their place he wished to create

[1] The 1952 treaty creating the ECSC and the Rome treaty of 1957.

'L'Europe des patries'—a loose confederation of separate national states. The *Rheinischer Merkur* pricked the de Gaulle bubble by writing: 'The Europe of national states . . . will be heralded with joy as a preliminary condition to unification, but it is only acceptable as a temporary makeshift.'

According to *Le Monde* of September 7th, London felt that de Gaulle's declarations had not dispelled doubts regarding possible diplomatic action which, in the British view, aimed at reorganising Europe in the form of a *third European force*, rejecting NATO, and whose leadership would be undertaken by President de Gaulle.

Next day *Le Monde* described the extent of the harm done to France: 'By and large the reactions abroad testify to the disquiet which the behaviour of the Chief of State has aroused, in restating his position all the more forcibly and calmly as it corresponds less and less with the ideas of his allies.'

The Times of September 7th is ironical: 'The spectacle of a head of state pressing along "the path of reason and justice", undeterred by critics at home or abroad is magnificent—but is it politics?'

The same day at Bonn, the Social Democratic opposition met and declared that de Gaulle 'has taken an axe to the very roots of NATO'. It asked the Chancellor 'how he imagined that he could ask the United States to protect Germany, while declaring himself in agreement with de Gaulle'.

One appreciates the predicament of the Chancellor, after the meeting at Rambouillet and after de Gaulle's press conference of September 5th.

On September 8th, on holiday at Cadenabbia, Adenauer was forced to announce: 'Obviously General de Gaulle's declarations have been wrongly interpreted, for he believes that only a coherent union of all the forces of all the free peoples can effectively withstand the Russian menace.' And he added: 'This union could not come about without the support of the United States.'

On September 13th de Gaulle received the Belgian Prime Minister and his Foreign Minister, after which the former announced to the press that his country would not admit any interference with the supranational organisations which already existed. Belgium was in favour of a European Community and against a Europe of separate national states. This shows the nature of the conversations which de Gaulle had had with his various foreign visitors. He wrote to me asking me to come and discuss Europe, NATO and the plan for a French striking force. I replied that I would willingly discuss Europe and NATO, but that I preferred to await the findings of a sub-committee of the Budget Commission before discussing the striking force.[1] I had a conversation with him before I left for Germany. He agreed that it was impossible to ask for a revision of the treaties dealing with Europe. I made a point of mentioning this to Adenauer.

On September 24th, at the Consultative Assembly of the European Council[2], most of the speakers declared that a Europe of national states is an anachronism.

For their part, the Christian Democrat deputies visited Chancellor Adenauer before the reopening of the German Parliament and said: 'You have led us three times to victory under the standard of Europe. We note that you are now in agreement with de Gaulle. In these circumstances would you kindly tell us under what flag we are now going to fight. For we feel bound to warn you that we shall all be defeated.'

It is easy to imagine the Chancellor's reaction. The Germans were, therefore, unanimous in their reaction against a Europe of national states.

On October 1st and 2nd, 1960, together with the members of the Finance Commission for military affairs, I visited the two French divisions attached to NATO. At all levels—troops, weapons and air cover—the entire situation was bad.

Visit to the Chancellor in Bonn.

On October 3rd I visited Chancellor Adenauer in Bonn. He received me in his drawing-room, seated at his big desk. On it I could see photographs which underlined the kindly nature of this resolute and upright fighter, whose face bears the stamp of bitter experience and which now showed the strain of the recent conversations at Rambouillet and their after-effects.

The Chancellor said that he was delighted to see me because in four days' time he would be receiving a visit from M. Debré, the French Prime Minister, and M. Couve de Murville, the Foreign Minister. He felt that the results of these conversations might be serious. He then explained the present state of affairs and his grievances. We discovered that we were completely in agreement and at his request I promised to give de Gaulle an unvarnished account of the situation.

[1] This invitation to discuss political problems with him was the only one I received.
[2] In 1938, this Council was formed which included representatives of the governments of the leading European nations. Subsequently, this Assembly was formed and comprised members elected by the parliaments of those countries belonging to the Council.

Unfortunately my walk on the previous day, across fields churned up by tanks, had not helped my knee, in which I had accidentally torn a muscle, although this had not then been discovered. As a result I had to take to my bed on my return to Paris and was unable to visit de Gaulle until after his Grenoble speech. But I asked Debré and Couve de Murville to come to see me and told them of my visit to the Chancellor and the seriousness of the tension between our two countries.

The Adenauer-Debre-Couve de Murville conversations.

The press had told us, or rather given us a hint, of what happened during the conversations of October 7th and 8th with the Chancellor.

On October 8th the headline of *Figaro* read: 'First stormy contact between the French and the Germans concerning the integration of the European forces.'

The French statesmen were conciliatory but the Chancellor, hearing that de Gaulle had just spoken in Grenoble, sent for a text of the speech, from which he singled out the following: 'If, by some calamity, atomic bombs are launched in the world, France intends that none should be launched from the side of the free world without her consent.' Such a defiant attitude could hardly be justified by the probabilities, for it would put an obstacle in the way of a prompt American reaction to defend us, whereas de Gaulle was the first to suspect them of refusing to do so for fear of reprisals.

'How can you reconcile this attitude with the assurances you have given me?' the Chancellor must have asked the two French ministers.

A communiqué was finally issued to the Press in which the Chancellor insisted that a passage should be included concerning relations with the United States. 'The closest cooperation between the European and North American partners of the Atlantic Alliance is the indispensable condition for an effective defence of the free world.'

We shall see that one characteristic of de Gaulle's policy is certainly not respect for any pledges taken in his name by his ministers.

The headlines of *Paris-Presse* the following day were very fair: 'Distrust between Paris and Bonn lessens but disagreement persists.' The communiqué had in fact carefully refrained from using the word 'integration'. And the same paper informed us that Debré had once more affirmed that French soldiers would only obey French officers, a nationalistic flourish which was impossible to justify since the Supreme Commander of NATO was an American.

The *Kölnischer Rundschau* laboured under a delusion when it wrote: 'France is aligning her position with that of her allies' although it added prudently: 'This affirmation will presumably remain valid . . . at least until another impromptu speech from General de Gaulle suddenly creates new *quid pro quos.*'

The truth is that frankness has not been a feature of Franco-German relations, by which each of the partners pretends to ignore the political philosophy of the other. *Combat* was therefore right in saying: 'Two concepts of Europe continue to conflict with each other.' One of them is sensible but alas it is not the one which we happen to support!

L'Express, on October 13th, displayed unwonted optimism by writing: 'M. Michel Debré, at the dictation of Chancellor Adenauer and common sense, has just renounced two years of Gaullist diplomacy.'

André François-Poncet, however, was circumspect when he wrote in *Le Figaro* of October 10th about the declarations made by de Gaulle on September 5th: 'Germany read into them his intention not only of dissociating himself from participation in the European enterprise but also . . . of taking a step backwards and endangering the results so far obtained.'

In October, 1962, when he visited Paris, Chancellor Adenauer gave a dinner at the Quai d'Orsay. After dinner I asked him: 'Where do we stand with Europe?' 'You will have to ask the General,' he replied. 'I believe, like the Spaniards, that advice and fresh water should only be given when asked for.' Questioned again, he replied: 'Yes, yes, you will have to ask the General!' The Chancellor had obviously given the green light for the Franco-German treaty.

Refusal to consider European integration, *even in the future*, is the fundamental cause of the split between de Gaulle and our partners. They want to build Europe. De Gaulle replies: 'Never!'

It is like painting imitation windows on a wall bearing the inscription in large letters: 'House of Europe'. He refuses to help build Europe, although we are involved in important schemes, both political and economical, throughout the world. We shall see how he brought the same attitudes of mind to bear on the Atlantic Alliance, where he alone was to oppose vital integration. In the same way, he challenged the United Nations, as he did not feel that it truly reflected national feelings. The same was to happen with Kennedy's Atlantic organisation.

Concerning Europe, de Gaulle is not a reactionary in the proper sense, for he is not asking for a return to the *status quo*. It is just that he refuses to go forward. He is like an enormous statue barring the road to the future. Our partners will bypass him one day and step out again on the road which Robert Schuman's France opened up. For, as the *New York Times* put it: 'The past cannot impose its veto on the future'.

January 19*th*, 1962, *de Gaulle torpedoes the Fouchet plan.*

De Gaulle's original 1961 plan concerning the framework of a European policy had two characteristics:
1. Hostility towards the technocrats of those European communities (ECSC, Common Market and Euratom) which are responsible for raising the standard of living of the six nations of the Common Market.
2. Hostility toward NATO, which integrates the forces of the members of the Atlantic alliance, and on which the security of Europe depends.

On these two essential points de Gaulle is in conflict with his five partners of the Common Market.

At Bonn on July 19th, 1961, de Gaulle made some compromises. He called off his attack on the European institutions, nor was there any further question of occasional meetings of defence ministers, with the object of tearing NATO to pieces.

On the other hand, de Gaulle got his way regarding a commission of *national* experts instructed to draw up proposals to be submitted at meetings of the heads of state or governments of the Six.

On October 19th, 1961, a plan was submitted to the commission— called the Fouchet Commission after its President, at that time our ambassador in Copenhagen, who played a very useful role in these negotiations.

The maintenance of the existing institutions was guaranteed in the preamble of the plan. It did not touch upon that part of the economic system deriving from European institutions.

A council composed of heads of states or governments was to meet three times a year. Three further meetings of foreign ministers would take place at intervals.

A political commission composed of high officials from the foreign ministries of the Six would sit.in Paris, each official being responsible, as we have seen, to his own government.

Decisions would be taken unanimously, at least for the first three years. Should a member of the council be absent at the time of voting, the decision would only apply to his country providing he consented.

Finally the European Parliament, created with the Common Market, could not pass a vote of censure against this council, but could do so against commissions entrusted with the management of European economic communities (Coal and Steel, Common Market, Euratom).

Unlike my friend, Jean Monnet, whom the Americans call the Father of Europe, and who has since told me that he has come round to my way of thinking, I was opposed from the very start to this plan, which did not contain a particle of true European spirit. This mistaken reform placed an obstacle in the path of the genuine reform that is essential for the creation of the political Europe which we so desperately need.

On January 19th, 1962, de Gaulle intervened.

Our five partners of the Common Market finally resigned themselves to accepting de Gaulle's plan. But the latter sent for the text drawn up by the Fouchet Commission and satisfied his hostility towards anything remotely European and to NATO by making six cuts or additions.

(1) The executives of the Commission must lose their autonomy.

(2) The organisations of the Common Market must be nationalised.

(3) The Council should be able to intervene on the subject of the defence of Europe.

(4) The Parliament should only put forward simple 'recommendations'.

(5) In the article concerning the revision of the statutes after three years, he suppressed the clause specifying that the existing structures be respected.

(6) He suppressed the clause which provided that in the revision of the statutes a supranational authority could be set up.

In addition to this de Gaulle berated his five partners in his televised speech of February 5th, 1962, in which he poured ridicule on the ideology of the 'Europeans' and the technocracy of the European institutions. Europe was still not a reality for him despite the success of the Common Market! It was an ideology. The Council he intended to control would have competence in economic matters. That is to say, it would have the means of attacking the European 'technocrats', and would have the power of dismantling the institutions created by the Treaty of Rome.

This time it was too much. The mask concealing so many declarations in favour of Europe had fallen.

Although he granted Chancellor Adenauer that the preamble to the treaty should contain a reference to NATO and that the Council could only discuss economic problems, within the framework of existing institutions, his refusal to admit that the European institutions could develop towards integration caused the setback to the meeting of the Six on April 17th, 1962.

41

Paul-Henri Spaak, for Belgium, and Joseph Luns for the Netherlands, were enthusiastic champions of integration. Since France made this impossible they turned towards Great Britain. Previously they would have opposed her entry into the Common Market because she had not been in favour of integration, until de Gaulle checked the progress towards Europe in the name of France! They also declared that they refused to negotiate on the future of Europe until the entry of Great Britain was accepted. The presence of Great Britain, said Messrs. Spaak and Luns, would at least have the advantage of balancing the Franco-German alliance. They did not know that de Gaulle would deprive this alliance of its content by this profound disagreement with Germany on all the main problems, and that they would soon see France alone and isolated.

The Fouchet Plan was abandoned. De Gaulle had killed it.

De Gaulle: Europe? simple cooperation!

This is how de Gaulle explained this rupture at his press conference of May 15th, 1962: 'Most of our partners would like this revision [of the stature of the European Economic Community] in the future to be effected in a supranational sense. *France still adheres to the formula of simple cooperation.*[1] On the other hand Belgium and the Netherlands, ready to abandon temporarily their integration hopes in the event of Great Britain entering the Common Market, refuse to continue negotiations until there are no further doubts about their joining.'

What of Europe? Simple cooperation! What about the federation and confederation? Vanished!

As we shall see, the French Chamber of Deputies signed by a large majority a declaration in favour of an integrated Europe the following month.

The representatives of the French people were in agreement with our five partners of the Common Market, but de Gaulle did not agree. And France lost.

We live under a system where a single man governs, and an irresponsible man at that!

What a picture of disorder we were treated to at his press conference. He should have added that his policy has already thrown Italy into the arms of Great Britain and that Germany unanimously demanded the admission of Great Britain into the Common Market. Since de Gaulle

[1] My italics.

was opposed to Britain's entry he should surely have clarified his position the year before, when Britain's candidature was on the agenda.

Alas, of all the Europeans on the continent de Gaulle has been the most hostile to a genuinely political Europe, for what can possibly be meant by 'simple cooperation'?

Who, therefore, rejects the solution desired by our five partners of the Common Market? France! France, which under the Fourth Republic was in this respect the leader of Europe!

Today, she brings up the rear and drags her feet. She could still have led Europe, but she refused.

To tell the truth, de Gaulle, who since then has spoken of Europe every time he makes a speech, continues the struggle against her which he began when he fought Robert Schuman. He refuses to admit the supranational authority which is the prerequisite for the existence of a United Europe. This caused the American Secretary of State, Mr Dean Rusk, to ask in Frankfurt in October, 1963: 'Where is Europe, then? Who speaks in her name?'

December, 1962, De Gaulle asks Macmillan: 'Do you choose Europe or America?'

Before travelling to meet Kennedy at Nassau, Macmillan saw de Gaulle.

The following account of events is taken from Roger Massip's valuable book *De Gaulle et l'Europe*, to which I have already referred several times in the course of this chapter.

'At Rambouillet, General de Gaulle strongly urged his guest to take sides for Europe by deciding to loosen once and for all the "special ties" existing between London and Washington. He told him quite bluntly that he did not believe Great Britain was ready to enter the European Community. In Mr Macmillan's actual words after the meeting: "He flung Winston Churchill at my head," a reference to Churchill's famous remark about Great Britain's traditional affinity with the open sea.[1] And finally he asked him point blank: "Are you capable of breaking with the United States and with the Commonwealth? Yes, or no?"'

Such a challenge seems unjustified, since all that President Kennedy had proposed was an association between America and a Europe, including Great Britain, who would thus become a partner with an authority equal to that of the United States.

[1] Churchill said to de Gaulle: 'If I were asked to choose between Europe and the open sea I should choose the open sea.'

A commission for foreign affairs and defence in Brussels.

'De Gaulle's plan has miscarried', I wrote on June 29th, 1962 in *Le Figaro*, in an article entitled: 'Europe deceased?' In this article I denounced the isolation of France and the basic contradictions in her policy—trying to fight against American preponderance and refusing to create a United Europe.

I pointed out that Great Britain was a candidate for the Common Market and, an aggravating circumstance, that she would not enter it alone. Denmark, Norway, Ireland and even Iceland were likely to be candidates and would perhaps enter in her train. The Common Market would in future have ten members instead of six. Under these conditions the rule of unanimity, which de Gaulle wished to impose on common decisions taken by representatives of these countries at the meetings he wished to organise, would have the effect of blocking the system. It would be enough for Ireland to say 'no' to a British proposal, for Iceland to say 'no' to a Danish proposal, for the proposal to be irrevocably rejected.

I recalled that the success of the Common Market Commission, with its headquarters in Brussels, was due to the fact that its members did not represent national interests but the interests of Europe; and I suggested the creation on the same pattern as Brussels of a Commission for Foreign Affairs and Defence.

After a trial period the rule of unanimity would continue to apply to suggestions put forward by one country. On the other hand, a suggestion made by the Commission could be voted by a qualified majority.[1] Obedience to the majority is the law of the democracies.

Would Great Britain agree to participate in a European policy? No one thought so at the time. Our Foreign Minister, Maurice Couve de Murville, declared before the National Assembly on July 13th, 1962, concerning the future of Europe: 'Everything depends on us knowing whether Great Britain will participate or not and, in her wake, a certain number of other countries.'

De Gaulle's passive France waited for England to decide her fate, at the same time deciding the fate of Europe . . .

In my article I demanded that France should act by putting to the vote the scheme I have just mentioned.

The following month Paul-Henri Spaak assembled about thirty European personalities in a castle near Brussels, and asked me to explain

[1] The larger nations having more votes than the smaller.

to them the scheme I had propounded in my *Figaro* article. The great majority were in favour of it.

M. Spaak passed on this suggestion to General de Gaulle. The reply, of course, was one more refusal: De Gaulle refused to budge from 'simple cooperation'.

On November 20th, 1963, M. Spaak repeated this idea in a statement made to the journalists attached to the European Community.

After the resounding success of the Brussels Commission in December, 1963 (which is described in Chapter 16), I am all the more keen to see the jurisdiction of it extended to foreign affairs and defence.

The Pope: European unity by actions.

Faced with the problem of Europe, as we shall see, and by the problem of the United Nations, we find the Vatican ahead of the Fifth Republic. On September 3rd, 1963, Pope Paul vi declared to the Congress of Catholic Universities: 'It is from now on the duty of the national societies which make up our continent to *resolve in a positive manner* the great question of European unity.

'We are convinced that the solution of the question admittedly demands *a series of measures of unification on various planes—economic, military and political*—but it also demands the creation of a unitarian mentality and a common culture.'

The following November 9th, Paul vi, after receiving me in private audience, said to the members of the Congress of the European Movement: 'Create Europe, otherwise someone else will do it in your place.'

The Pope is a man of the 20th century.

A man of what was.

The Europe which de Gaulle wanted then to create bears a closer resemblance to the Holy Alliance concluded between the Allied sovereigns after Waterloo than to the integrated Europe which our five partners of the Common Market wish to realise.

In the Holy Alliance, which was signed in September, 1815, we read: 'The sole principle in force between the signatories shall be to render mutual service, to show unfailing goodwill and mutual affection, to consider themselves as *members of a single Christian nation*, the three princes merely seeing themselves as delegates chosen by Providence to govern three branches of a single family.'

45

They agreed to meet in congress at certain fixed periods to study *'great common interests and the measures which during each of these periods should be considered as most salutary for the tranquillity and prosperity of the nations and for the maintenance of peace in Europe.'*

Naturally the rule of unanimity, so dear to de Gaulle, applied, but the accent was warmer than that of 'simple cooperation' beyond which de Gaulle has declared he will not go.

This pact could perhaps have been the blueprint for an organisation of the United States of Europe had not Metternich, who called himself 'a man of what was' used it as a weapon with which to fight the ideas of the revolution and the national and liberal movements.

The 'man of what was' is the part played today by de Gaulle, whose ambition is confined to trying to imitate the occasional meetings of Metternich's Europe and his rule of unanimity.

Our kings, in days gone by, created France and her provinces by means of the sword and by marriages. Today, the nations must create Europe progressively by means of mutual understanding.

By opposing integration, de Gaulle is today playing against Europe the role of a feudal baron of the Middle Ages, who fought with the sword against the king to prevent the integration which resulted in France.

CHAPTER 3

De Gaulle opposes a common European defence policy and urges a French striking force

'We have pursued a policy of self-esteem instead of one of security.'
PAUL REYNAUD,
National Assembly, November 9th, 1961.

THIS IS HOW I SUMMED UP THE MILITARY POLICY OF THE FIFTH REPUB-LIC in the debate on the creation of a French striking force. Let us have a look at the details of the problem.

We are part of the Western world. In 1948, Soviet Russia, the only great military power in Europe, consolidated her hold on Czechoslovakia. Was there anything to halt the advance of Communism westwards? This was the question asked by an anxious Europe. America then played her role as leader of the free world. Together with the countries of Western Europe she founded NATO.

Two years later I campaigned against the inadequacy of the European military effort compared with that of the United States, as outlined by General Omar Bradley, Chairman of the Joint Chiefs of Staff of the United States.

On July 21st, 1950, I attended a meeting in support of a United Europe at the Albert Hall before an audience of six or seven thousand people, with Winston Churchill presiding. I said to this audience: 'What is the balance sheet? What have we to set against 175 Russian divisions? A phantom army; a dozen or so divisions, several of which are far below strength and equipped with obsolete material.'

Five days later in the House of Commons, Churchill questioned Emanuel Shinwell, the Minister of War in the Labour Government: 'M. Reynaud . . . made some precise statements on this point [the strength of the Western Union] last week . . . I should think he is tolerably well-informed on these matters . . . Was he more or less right?'

Since Mr Shinwell did not reply to this question, Churchill interrupted him and put the question a second time. The Minister did not dispute my figures for very good reasons.

The *Economist* wrote that these revelations had produced the same effect as the news released after Munich—that Great Britain was unarmed.

Seven days after the Albert Hall meeting I produced these same figures in the French Chamber. Jules Moch, the Minister for National Defence, interrupted me in these terms: 'I do not know whether it is a very good thing to say this in the House, as you have done, considering the authority attaching to your name.'

To which I replied: 'I think it is a very good thing to tell the people the truth.'

It will be seen, therefore, that my disagreement with the authorities on military matters began before the return of de Gaulle in 1958.

1959. *France will wage war 'in her own fashion'.*

In 1950 de Gaulle took his stand on the problem of the defence of Europe, at the time when the Atlantic Alliance was established by the United States with an American Supreme Commander. Still intent upon excluding the Anglo-Saxons, as he calls them nowadays, so that France might be 'in the forefront', he declared at his press conference of August 17th, 1950: 'We have to rally Europe . . . We need in fact a common system of defence in which France's natural function is *to draw up the plans and to appoint the leader*, just as this pre-eminence devolves upon the United States *in the Pacific and upon Great Britain in the Far East*.'

It is no longer 'Yankees go home!' but 'Go to the Pacific!' That's even farther away.

Had the Americans followed this advice instead of exerting herself in organising Europe with the stupendous resources at her disposal, the Russians might have advanced to Brest.

American, French, British, German and other forces were integrated in NATO. Under the orders of an American Supreme Commander, a general staff was set up, composed of officers from the allied armies.

On his return to power de Gaulle revealed his basic principles in his famous conference on November 2nd, 1959, to the School of Advanced Military Studies. They were diametrically opposed to those of NATO.
(1) 'The defence of France must be French.
(2) 'It is essential that France defends herself, by herself, and in her own fashion . . .

(3) 'If a nation like France has to wage war it must be *her* war and any war effort must be *her* effort. Were it otherwise it would be at variance with all our country has stood for since its origins, with its role in history, its self esteem and its spirit . . . This system of integration has survived.'

These words must be read with one's own eyes to be believed.

Thus the head of the French state raised the standard of revolt against NATO. It was a break with the very organisation of the alliance he himself had demanded. It was a refusal to accept the self-discipline incumbent upon these various countries if they wished to combine their efforts to safeguard their independence.

On reading these words one cannot help thinking that it was just in this way that the peoples of Ancient Greece lost their liberty.

It is difficult to believe that these quotations are accurate. 'In *her* fashion', '*her* war'! Since, before invading France, the Russian army would first have to contend with the NATO army in Germany, including our two divisions, did he not see that such a war could only be European in scope?

The words he uttered were so serious, and this determination to return to the old formula of collaboration between independent national armies (each one retaining freedom of action) so contrary to the very concept of NATO that the French General Valluy, formerly Commander of the Central European forces, publicly stated that to maintain the morale of the officers under his command he was forced quite frankly to take the opposite view. Since then de Gaulle has never missed an opportunity of airing his theory, appealing to the vanity and the jingoistic spirit of the French people to incite them against integration.

We shall see de Gaulle cling to this extraordinary military doctrine which brings him into conflict with all our Allies, just as his extraordinary doctrine for Europe places him in the opposite camp to all our partners of the Common Market.

At his press conference of April 11th, 1961, he asserted: 'It is intolerable for a great state to have its fate left to the decisions and actions of another state.' But the fate of France is bound up with the fate of Europe, since a war between France and Russia alone is unthinkable.

And de Gaulle added: 'Furthermore, integration results in the integrated country being induced to lose interest in its national defence since it is no longer responsible for it.' If each country in Europe reasoned in the same way, Europe would be in a sorry state. The results of this refusal to create Europe are plain to see.

At his press conference of July 29th, 1961, de Gaulle repeated this unreasonable demand. To the reproaches levelled at his predecessors, he was now to add this grievance against the Europe which they wanted to see united: '*It was the same thing with NATO, where the responsibility for the defence of our country was in the hands of an American military command.*'

But here too it was a question of the defence of Europe, of which our country is a part, and not of the defence of France alone. Surely we should congratulate ourselves that the Americans are committed to it through the responsibility of the Supreme Command? For us this spells salvation, for in fact a defeat in Europe would be a defeat for the United States. Besides, is it not normal in any alliance for the command to go to the ally whose contribution is the greatest? This is why the command was given to the French General Foch at the end of the First World War. What if our allies had answered in 1918: 'We intend to wage war in our own fashion'? In 1945 the Supreme Commander was Eisenhower. In his attitude de Gaulle is literally a reactionary. Today the Americans, quite apart from their six modern divisions, have the most powerful nuclear force in the world. How could we dream of claiming the command when our contribution is so weak in relation to theirs? We are very weak in conventional[1] weapons, our nuclear weapons were non-existent in 1961 and, until recently, ridiculously inadequate. Besides, have we the military and financial means of organising the defence of Europe?

One is dumbfounded at such pretensions. Had the Americans, with the approval of all the other allies, said: 'So be it. Take your two divisions and defend France,' should we have accepted?

How could we possibly do it with only these two divisions of outdated heavy tanks (later to be withdrawn from NATO) and the divisions brought back from Algeria, against thousands of Russian rockets and H-bombs, plus whatever might be left of their modern and motorised divisions after they had clashed with the NATO army?

De Gaulle's attitude towards NATO is even less defensible since France's signature is set against the Atlantic Treaty which calls for *economic* collaboration (Article 2) and *political* consultation (Article 4). This was no 19th century alliance. In 1956 the Council of NATO created institutions designed to animate these arrangements. But since de Gaulle's return to power France has adopted towards NATO an attitude which, to say the least, is uncooperative. Dr Dirk U. Stikker, Secretary General of NATO, has implicitly condemned it, as we shall see.

[1] As opposed to atomic.

To those who shrink from the idea of integration I would point out that the Soviet defence budget is inferior to the combined defence budget of the allies. Nevertheless, Soviet efficiency, which is due to unified command, has allowed them to maintain and even to increase their crushing supremacy in conventional divisions, airfields and submarines. Even with the enormous expense of these conventional forces Russia has caught up with America in the atomic field and has overtaken her in the space programme!

In Western Europe, there is no concerted system of logistics. To decide against integration is to decide against efficiency; a prerequisite for security.

And while de Gaulle refuses integration into NATO, we have the anomaly of German and French soldiers training side by side by virtue of the Franco-German Treaty! The Gaullists who heard General de Montsabert, one of their most active leaders, wax indignant in the Salle Wagram at the very idea that a German soldier could set foot on French soil, must have been somewhat embarrassed. We of the opposition felt not the slightest embarrassment.

De Gaulle's attitude towards NATO was to lead inevitably, as will be seen, to a desire for his own private striking force.

I was to speak to him later on the subject of these conventional forces.

July 11th, 1961. I write to de Gaulle asking him to invite Europe to do her duty.

On July 11th, 1961, twenty-eight days before Berlin was cut in two and in the course of a fact-finding trip, I wrote to de Gaulle, expressing my anxiety: 'For six months as many refugees have left East Germany via Berlin as during the preceding twelve months. This silent plebiscite is harmful both to Pankow[1] and to Moscow.' I concluded that there was a serious threat of this exodus from East to West being curtailed. 'Now,' I added, 'General Norstad'—at that time NATO Commander-in-Chief —'has just stated that "the forces of the Atlantic Alliance are insufficient to fulfil all their commitments".' What an indictment before history of those European allies, whom he and his predecessors had so often warned that the soil on which they tread would or could be invaded.

I then pointed out that President Kennedy had announced in a declaration to Congress that his country would increase its efforts in the field of *conventional* weapons, and I added: 'Western Europe, the most interested party, which is more heavily populated and wealthier than

[1] The capital of East Germany.

Russia, is not doing its duty.' I concluded: 'You alone are qualified to show Europe in your forthcoming speech that the only adequate reply to Khruschev is to achieve unity and to arm without a moment's delay.'

But de Gaulle was only thinking of his striking force, and did not want to create Europe . . . Twenty-eight days later, Berlin was sliced in two. The allies did not react.

Why our allies ask us to create conventional divisions.

The Americans have sensibly pointed out that the effect of an atomic war would be so appalling and so final that everything must be done to prevent a local clash, which could well develop into a genocidal war. In order to meet an attack made with purely conventional weapons, we must be in a position to resist with the same conventional weapons. The use of nuclear weapons would, of course, be tantamount to suicide and we should always give the enemy time to reflect, and hope he would think twice before destroying his own people.

This is the idea of the 'escalade', of successive stages of warfare.

Europe has been able to survive a conventional war; she would not survive nuclear war. Mistakes would be even more costly than last time. The penalty for an error in policy could mean the death of a whole nation. Let us not forget that today there are many flashpoints which could lead to war: Berlin, Cuba, and, to a lesser degree, Vietnam and Laos. Nor, above all, do we know who will succeed Khruschev.

At present, NATO has not enough conventional divisions to resist without going a stage further and using tactical nuclear weapons. The Americans have told us frankly that we cannot expect a greater effort from Germany, which already has twelve modern conventional divisions in NATO. Therefore, they are calling upon us.

France refuses the effort demanded of her by her allies.

In 1952, at the Lisbon Conference[1], France promised to bring to the alliance fourteen modern divisions, so as to have a larger force than the twelve divisions envisaged for West Germany. Because of the Algerian war, France could not honour her commitments. But even when this war was over, NATO was only granted the use of two French divisions whose heavy tanks, as I have said, were obsolete. Surely we could at least have made the effort requested of us—to create *modern* conventional

[1] This conference apportioned the military forces to be allotted to NATO by each Ally.

divisions. Only the modern American and German divisions can possibly balance the corresponding Russian divisions. The Russians have twenty-five of these on the frontiers of Central Europe against six American and twelve German divisions.

While asserting that the allies are stronger than the Russians in all fields—this, I think, is to overlook the huge Soviet reserves—Mr Mac-Namara, United States Secretary of Defence, ended his speech of November 19th, 1963, to the Economic Club of New York, with these words: 'All this does not mean to say that the land forces of NATO in Europe are sufficient to defeat a surprise attack without the aid of nuclear weapons.' (An allied leader said to me that the Russians could, in fact, take Hamburg in a single raid.) Mr MacNamara added that his country had played its part and it was up to the allies to do the same.

We are extremely well placed to bring to this association valuable human capital: our reserves are well-trained, particularly in the field of communications, and are capable of using all the modern equipment of conventional armoured divisions.

The problem of France's effective contribution is very acute. Should the Republicans come to power in the United States, it is possible that they would support the views of their ex-President, Eisenhower, who is in favour of withdrawing from Europe all the American divisions except one.

On November 15th, 1963, Premier Pompidou boasted that he had refused to give our allies the conventional divisions they had requested. He said: 'If we created the armoured divisions which our allies demand, it would cost us at least as much and we should be less well defended.'

It is true that it would be very expensive, but this expenditure would allow us to bring an effective contribution to the common cause, whereas the contribution of our atomic force, to which he alludes, would be ridiculous in comparison with that of our allies and catastrophic for us, *as we shall see.*

Our Premier, like his chief, is obviously haunted by the idea of a war which everyone wages 'in his own fashion'.

Now let us take a look at the main complaints that are levelled against us. As soon as he came to power, de Gaulle withdrew from NATO our Mediterranean fleet, which constituted the main part of the joint allied forces in that area. In June, 1963, de Gaulle withdrew from NATO the French Atlantic fleet. Concerning the land forces, I have already mentioned France's two NATO divisions, whose tanks date back to the last war.

53

Although propaganda from certain quarters accuses the Americans of trying to make the French the 'black sheep' of NATO, we are generally regarded as a bad ally. None of this prevented de Gaulle from declaring at a press conference, televised on July 29th, 1963: 'France is modernising her army, is equipping it herself and is on the way to acquiring her own nuclear power.' He also formally condemned integration of military forces, though well aware that NATO is based on it! Kennedy replied a few days later at his press conference that integration was indispensable. Thus disagreement was now total and undisguised.

And that is not all. President Kennedy affirmed at Frankfurt on June 25th, 1963, that America would honour her commitments towards her allies. (We shall see de Gaulle casting doubts on the execution of this pledge.)

One cannot help asking the following question: ' If there were two de Gaulles in Europe, would the American army waste any time in returning home?'

This is a very real question, for Kennedy warned us some months ago not to reawaken American isolationism; and recent remarks by influential members of Congress are threatening enough.

There are already signs of a gradual withdrawal. We learnt on September 30th, 1963, when the Americans air-lifted their 2nd Armoured Division into Germany for manoeuvres, of a reorganisation of their pattern of logistics in Europe, mainly with a view to dispensing with France. The press assured us that this was not a punitive gesture directed against France, but simply a demonstration that the geographical 'primacy' of France no longer existed. Americans, infuriated with the uncooperative attitude of France, must have been relieved to hear the news. In future, the advanced American aerial bridgeheads in Europe will be Bremerhaven, Hanau and Frankfurt.

American public opinion.

It should be emphasised that de Gaulle's attitude towards the problem of the common defence of Europe has hardly gone unnoticed in the United States. For example, the American magazine *Life*, with a circulation of 7 million, published in November, 1963, an article entitled, 'The NATO Alliance Is In Danger'. The article quoted de Gaulle's declaration to Macmillan: 'France will be in it [NATO] less and less.' According to the author of this article, the fact that de Gaulle has withdrawn the French Mediterranean and Atlantic fleets, and refuses to fulfil France's commitments concerning her armed forces, shows his absolute contempt for NATO. Although, his article continues, his attitude is partly attributable to the US refusal to relax its 'monopoly grip on NATO's nuclear defence' and to admit other nations to a more equal standing within the alliance.

When the Council of Ministers of NATO met in Paris the *New York Times* of December 16th, 1963, stated that de Gaulle offered the delegates on their arrival 'a bitter aperitif'. In fact, after the shock caused by the assassination of President Kennedy, the representatives of all the other nations were hopeful of confirming their unity and complete solidarity; but they were forced to take note that de Gaulle was in total disagreement with NATO strategy, declaring that the theory of the 'escalade' was absurd and that the immediate response to any form of aggression would be suicidal war.

At this meeting of NATO the French Minister for Foreign Affairs declared once more that if the Americans and the British wanted to talk to Khruschev, this was their business, but France refused to do so.

It is worth stressing that this occurred immediately after the Moscow Treaty and the announcement made by the Soviet leader on the eve of the NATO meeting that he was about to cut down his military expenditure.

One of the outstanding features of de Gaulle's character is his persistence in making political decisions with no regard for events.

So France will remain alone.

The crucial question: can France afford the nuclear weapon?

Let us remember that Great Britain, a richer nation than we are, which has had no expenses comparable to those we incurred in Algeria, and who has made fewer financial sacrifices for her former African colonies than we have for ours and for Madagascar, has had the H-bomb for twelve years (1952). Yet she still does not possess the rocket to deliver it on target. At his Bahamas meeting with Kennedy, Macmillan had to accept another form of American aid in the shape of Polaris, for the Americans refused to finance the tests which were needed to equip the British air force with Skybolt, an air-to-ground missile.

De Gaulle reproached Macmillan for having accepted this proposal, but made no offer to substitute French aid for American; if a striking force is so expensive to perfect that even Great Britain, rich as she is, finds herself in need of aid, what kind of contribution could France

55

make? Mr Khruschev told Mr Harold Wilson, leader of the British Labour Party, that Russia had abandoned bomb-carrying aircraft because of their vulnerability. This will be our plight until we possess the rocket, and nobody can say when that will be.

The nuclear race between the two great powers is a hellish one. Tomorrow they will be able to stop the enemy's rockets, and the day after tomorrow they will send satellites into space capable of carrying nuclear warheads which can be exploded at any given point on the earth.

Does de Gaulle really believe that, in the throes of this race, Khruschev is going to sit down at the roadside and wait for us? We shall always lag behind. Admittedly, the modern weapon is the nuclear weapon, but it can only be employed by those powers which have sufficient waste spaces in which to perfect their weapons and all the resources of a great continent. To give an example: our air alert system is directly dependent on NATO, so not even on this crucial point can we pretend to be independent.

A French striking force would lead to catastrophe.

Certain people are surprised that today, having always wanted France to assume leadership, I reject the nuclear weapon for the French army. Isn't an army without nuclear weapons hopelessly old-fashioned? The situation could be contrasted, so the argument might run, with 1940, when the army was accused of being deficient—both in armoured divisions and in assault aircraft.

I want to explain myself clearly. France must have chairs of science and she must have laboratories. She must produce nuclear energy for her industries. Her scientists must continue research in the nuclear field.

Official spokesman appeal to their countrymen thus: 'Are you criticising the striking force? Do you want France to be a backward nation? Don't you see that, thanks to the efforts we are making to get it, we are building a generation of research workers who will keep France in her rightful place?'

Alas, an enquiry carried out in January, 1964,[1] among scientists and qualified research workers, confirmed that this statement is entirely false; they are unanimously opposed to a striking force that will use up to 60% of our research scientists and whose work on nuclear weapons will be of no scientific interest. They say: 'From the scientific point of

[1] *Le Figaro Littéraire*, January 30th, 1964.

view, it is as if one were to remove 60% of our urgently-needed young research workers to build, in great secrecy, a crossbow factory!' One of them added: 'If too many of our scientists were diverted from science by this crossbow factory we would soon find ourselves overtaken, in the scientific field, by Egypt!'

Be that as it may, Europe lives today under the terrible threat (even if improbable) of total destruction. So a bucket brigade must be formed, as at a fire. The United States now has a nuclear force superior in certain respects to that of the Soviet Union. She has more than 2000 nuclear stockpiles, according to the statement made by Mr MacNamara on December 17th, 1963, to the Council of NATO ministers. Our own contribution to the Atlantic community in this field would be insignificant compared with American nuclear power, nor could we make it for some years to come. These are the facts.

Now what would a striking force cost us? The third Pierrelatte factory, which is exclusively engaged at present in manufacturing the hydrogen bomb, will cost us more than 500,000 million old francs, and 50,000 million annually in running costs.

But I must stress again that it is not enough to make the bomb. We have to be able to deliver it on target. Hence the offer of the American Polaris, accepted in principle by Germany and Britain but refused by us. We should fight, therefore, with bomb-carrying aircraft against rockets!

Will the effort be worth-while? No! For compared with the stockpiles accumulated by the United States, our contribution to the Community will be practically nil, as we have seen.

De Gaulle boasted in one of his press conferences that France could despatch them to any part of the globe.

This ability is of dubious practical value. The Americans did not use them in Korea. During the Suez adventure (which I opposed unsuccessfully before the National Assembly) Britain possessed the H-bomb, but the idea of using it never entered her head. The whole world would have been up in arms had she done so. Since a war between Russia and France alone is inconceivable, we can only think in terms of a war between Russia and Europe. These are the only circumstances in which the atomic bomb could be used. But as we have seen, if the Americans use theirs our nuclear contribution would be negligible. Furthermore, because of the small extent of our territory compared with that of Russia—which stretches from 60 miles east of the Rhine to Vladivostock—the first bomb dropped on Russian soil would bring immediate retaliation. Within a few minutes the Soviet Union's medium range rockets would wipe France off the map. They would not even have to use their long-range rockets, capable of reaching the United States.

Unfortunately it would not be a matter of complete annihilation. Those who died instantly would be the lucky ones. The injuries sustained by untold numbers of men, women and children would be appalling. The few unscathed survivors would give birth to degenerates.

But, some people say, our atomic force, however weak, would make it possible for us to bring pressure to bear on the Americans to unleash a nuclear war!

Let us be serious. There is no proof that it would force the Americans to do so. The only thing that is certain is that if we unleashed nuclear war by attacking Russia we should be destroyed instantly. Therefore, if the Americans were to launch a nuclear attack in response to our appeal, they would be bringing aid to a corpse.

This is what the Frenchman, responsible for pressing the atomic button, would have to consider. An order—it is nearly a law—has decided that this person would be the President of the Republic. This, let it be said in passing, is a new violation of the Constitution, in view of the fact that it is the Prime Minister who is personally responsible for national defence.

The official French theory is that the Russians do not fear an avalanche of rockets and hydrogen bombs, because they believe that America would not dare use them for fear of seeing some of her own cities destroyed. On the other hand, we are told, they stand in dread of the new French atom bomb-carrying aircraft, believing that France, although aware that she would die on the spot, would not hesitate to despatch them.

Is this reasonable?

It would no longer be national defence but national suicide—and all this in order to be registered as a 'member of the Atomic Club'! This is where our ambition to be treated as a 'great power' would lead us, and this is why we are not doing our duty as an ally, by refusing to create modern conventional divisions.

Purely as a matter of prestige, is it not obvious that America attaches far more importance to the twelve German divisions than to the British bombs? Then, too, there are several classes in the Atomic Club. France, in any case, would only be a third-class member. Great Britain who, unlike us, has the hydrogen bomb but no rockets, would belong to the second class. On his south-eastern tour in September, 1963, de Gaulle repeatedly stated that he would not admit that *two* powers should have the monopoly of the nuclear weapon. He did not even pay Great Britain the compliment of mentioning her once.

So whereas France could make a very useful contribution to the defence of the West, she refuses to do this simply because she recoils from the idea of submitting to a form of discipline which our common salvation demands, and wants to be able to boast the possession of a bomb which she could never use under pain of immediate death. For France does not possess any conventional defence forces at all. The conclusion is that once more, as before 1870, 1914 and 1939, we have shown ourselves incapable of preparing for a threatened war.

This is why France was not represented at Moscow and did not share the joy which all the nations of the world felt at the time.

A return to France's traditional policy.

Our ministers sometimes ask: 'Would another government, representing the views of today's opposition, be able to stop the nuclear programme now that it is under way?' But this is asking the wrong question. What France should do is to radically change her entire policy with regard to NATO, the United States, and the world.

This hypothetical government should say to the President of the United States: 'We are resolute supporters of integration, in the true spirit of NATO. We are ready to return to that organisation the French Mediterranean and Atlantic fleets, which have been withdrawn, and to bring to it all the divisions at our disposal, as Germany has already done. In short, we will be loyal and cooperative allies. The power of your nation does not terrify us: on the contrary, it reassures us for, as President Kennedy said at Frankfurt, your feeling of moral solidarity with Europe is in your own interests.

'Furthermore, there have been developments in the world. 650 million Chinese now challenge 220 million Russians. This is a fact to be taken into account.

'We are prepared to subscribe to the Moscow Treaty, wishing to associate ourselves with all the other nations who see in it a sign of hope. We will also sign any agreement with the Russians, mutually undertaking to refrain from aggression, after discussing the terms with you and Great Britain.

'For your part we expect that, having openly shown us the scope of your nuclear power, you will accept the consequence which France's new attitude entails—in other words, that you share your nuclear information with us.'

So the prodigal son would return to the great family of the democracies!

Can we be certain we should receive immediate satisfaction? The Americans might hesitate since the Germans, who as we have seen are model associates, would also insist on reaping the benefit of this royal gift. The most probable hypothesis would be a European-type solution which, for the reasons I have given, would involve collaboration with the United States for some time to come. A few French ultra-nationalists might protest, but our prestige in the world would be considerably increased. It is true that in order to bring this about we should have to help to create Europe, but who would prevent us from doing so? But we should have to hurry, to make up for the time lost under the Fifth Republic.

We would make progress in the scientific field, and we could make the effort demanded of us in the field of conventional weapons. One day we could lead a European striking force, including Great Britain. But until then it is America alone who can safeguard us in the atomic field.

This, you will say, would be a complete reversal of today's actual policies. Yes, a complete reversal!

CHAPTER 4 *No conversations
with Khruschev*

On August 13th, Berlin is cut in two.

ON JULY 10TH, 1961, IN MOSCOW, ADDRESSING THE STUDENTS OF THE
Soviet Military Academy, Mr Khruschev declared: 'We invite President
Kennedy, General de Gaulle and Prime Minister Macmillan to come
and sit round a conference table with the other peace-loving nations
and to conclude a peace treaty . . . After a peace treaty has been signed,
the USSR will renounce all the obligations she has so far assumed on
the West Berlin lines of communication.' He meant of course Western
Germany's access to West Berlin, a storm-tossed island in a Communist
sea. Khruschev also said that in view of the increase in the military
budgets of NATO, the Soviet Union would follow suit. But it was a
a courteous invitation.

Four days later, on July 14th, General de Gaulle replied to his offer
in these terms: 'As I have often had the occasion to say, particularly
last year in Paris to President Kennedy, if the Russians sincerely want,
as they maintain, an easing of tension and co-existence, let them begin
to make this possible by ceasing to utter threats.'

Following French advice, the allies rejected Mr Khruschev's proposal. A month later, on August 13th, Berlin was cut in two by the wall.
The allies bowed to the inevitable. This was the result of the policy of
refusing to talk.

To allay the anxiety of the Berliners, President Kennedy sent his
Vice-President, Lyndon Johnson, who pledged 'the sacred honour of
the United States' that the freedom of their lines of communication
with the West would continue to be guaranteed. This consisted in the

main of three air corridors used by aircraft arriving from or returning to Federal Germany.

On the following September 2nd, Mr Khruschev sent the allies a note in which he alleged that these air corridors were being used for 'spies, warmongers and seekers of revenge'. Recalling that American honour had been pledged, I felt that the risk of war was very great.

My interview with Khruschev.

Through Maurice Dejean, our ambassador in Moscow, I requested an audience with Mr Khruschev with whom, three years previously, I had had a two-hour conversation. I was agreeably surprised by the Premier's reply: 'I shall be happy to have a conversation at such a high level.' For on the eve of the day fixed for our conversation, Marshal Malinowsky, Soviet Minister for Defence, had stated that the Russian Army possessed bombs equivalent to several million tons of TNT and concluded: 'We must hold ourselves in readiness for a terrible and bitter war.' The threat of war was certainly growing daily. Certain people wondered—as de Gaulle did publicly—whether the Supreme Head of the Soviet Union had not chosen the path of catastrophe to conceal some internal crisis.

At the end of a long table in Mr Khruschev's study, round which the ministers and leaders of the Communist Party often sat, I came face to face with one of the two most powerful men in the world.

Our conversation lasted three hours. I said to him: 'This is the first time since the "great terror" of the year A.D. 1000[1] that the white race fears that it will disappear, but this time there is some foundation for its fear. I am going to tell you what the West thinks of you. Its view is that you are intoxicated by the successes of Communism which you have seen spread to China in the East, to Cuba in the West, to North Korea in the North and to North Vietnam in the South, and that you are also intoxicated by the successes of Gagarin and Titov. In brief, intoxicated in just the same way as Kaiser Wilhelm II and Hitler. Like them, it is said, you want to put back the clock of history. They also say that you will end up as they did.

'My personal opinion is quite different. I believe you realise that the name of the man who unleashes the suicidal war of the white race will be execrated until the end of time, starting with the few survivors and their degenerate progeny. Besides, you are a statesman, you look to the

[1] Devout Christians persuaded themselves that this year would mark the end of the world.

future, and you know that the man who would sit in your chair after such a war would be Chinese.'

'You said much the same to me three years ago,' he replied in a calm, serious voice.

To his question: 'Why are you a European?' I had at that time replied: 'Because before the turn of the century there will be a thousand million Chinese.'

Now I added: 'You would be like a chess player who on the point of winning the game knocks over the chess board.'

Mr Khruschev admitted that the danger of war was very great.

'What is at stake?' I asked. 'The Berliners' right of access to the West. Is there a peasant anywhere in the world, whose land is enclosed, who does not have the right to cross his neighbour's land to reach his own farm? Do you intend to destroy your people in order to deprive West Berlin of such an elementary right? How would you be judged by history if you caused the white races to annihilate each other merely for a right of way? Make no mistake, Kennedy, with whom I talked this spring, is a brave man. He would not allow it to be said of him that under his Presidency the United States was deficient in a sense of honour. Moreover, public opinion urges him forward instead of holding him back. A Gallup poll[1] has just proved this.

'What need is there for a war? Because of those who seek revenge? Where are their rockets to accomplish this revenge? Because of spies? Every nation, including yours, employs spies.'

Khruschev agreed that the question of peace was a matter of urgency and admitted that war would be suicidal.

After a long discussion on the right of access and the recognition of East Germany, to which the West cannot agree, I asked him: 'Do you really think it would be wise to place the choice of peace or war in the hands of the men of Pankow?' Khruschev's defence of his subordinates was brief and half-hearted.

Finally Khruschev said to me: 'While I am the leader of this great socialist country, it will not be the two million inhabitants of West Berlin who will decide whether your form of government or mine will prevail. Our competition will be settled in a far wider sphere. West Berlin is only a drop in the ocean, incapable of tipping the scales in either direction. All that matters is: which social system will triumph in the course of history?' To which I replied: 'How pleasant it is to hear words of such good sense.' Our conversation ended on the friendliest

[1] July, 1961.

note. His parting shot as he left me was: 'Give my regards to your pupil!'

From his opening statement that the question of war and peace was a matter of urgency, to his admission that West Berlin was only a drop in the ocean, was a far cry!

After having arranged for this conversation to be published in *Le Figaro* of September 23rd, 1961[1], I replied as follows to the policy of 'No talks with Mr Khruschev':

'Let us be careful not to isolate France.

'An attitude which rightly or wrongly appears indirectly to blame the United States for having agreed to negotiate, for I am incapable of distinguishing between putting out feelers and negotiating, does not seem to be in France's best interests.

'The position we have already taken, although possibly wrongly interpreted, has made us appear as the Western nation most hostile to Soviet Russia. *Izvestia* has accused us of having 'forgotten everything'. This attitude might have dire consequences if war, which is still a possibility, were to break out.

'To stand aloof from these negotiations, to say nothing of repudiating them, would give America the right to settle the fate of the free world on her own, in a *tête à tête* with Soviet Russia.

'Isolation would spell decline.'

Three days later, Mr Khruschev received M. Paul-Henri Spaak, the Belgian Minister for Foreign Affairs, and told him that he would withdraw his ultimatum, which had been couched in the following terms:

'Unless an agreement is reached between the allies, East Germany and myself over Berlin before the end of 1961, I will sign a separate treaty with Communist East Germany.'

This, as I said to Mr Khruschev, would have placed the choice of peace or war in the hands of the leaders of East Germany.

Khruschev has still not presented the allies with a new ultimatum.

This, I think, proves that personal contact with him can prove useful in spite of what is maintained in Paris.

Shortly after my return from Russia, I learned—for everything leaks out in the Fifth Republic as in all other countries—that I had been accused in the Council of Ministers[2] of having been too optimistic in my account in *Le Figaro* of my conversation with Mr Khruschev, and of having taken too weak a stand towards him. However, Kruschev's with-

[1] Since then I have met the Russian interpreter, today employed in Paris, who congratulated me on the accuracy of my account of this interview.
[2] The Cabinet, presided over by de Gaulle.

drawal of his ultimatum provided solid grounds for my optimism, though I did not know it at the time.

As for my conversation, which allegedly had weakened America's negotiating position, this is how I ended my account in *Le Figaro*:

'Negotiation does not mean capitulation, and there is no reason to think that in his present conversations with Mr Gromyko, Mr Dean Rusk will show himself to be any less explicit than I was myself towards Mr Khruschev on the subject of freedom of communication between West Berlin and the West.' Had I weakened the Americans? This is how I concluded the talk I gave on my return on CBS, one of America's television networks: 'This conversation [with Mr Khruschev] made me hope that peace can be preserved provided that President Kennedy and the American people continue to show Mr Khruschev that they are not prepared to surrender in the face of force and terror.'

That is how I weakened the Americans!

The Council of Ministers was certainly very hard to please . . .

A month after my return I met de Gaulle at a Ministry of the Interior cocktail party. He made a disparaging remark about my conversation with Mr Khruschev, to which I replied, just as curtly.

Before my visit to Germany, a year earlier, I had said to him on this subject: 'If you persist in refusing to talk to Mr Khruschev it will be Kennedy, Macmillan and he who, in your absence, will decide the fate of France, Europe and the world.'

He had replied with an observation which sounded so disillusioned that it surprised me to hear it from his lips: 'They will do that in any case . . . ' I do not believe that this would happen.

President Kennedy, profiting from the lesson of Berlin, was wise enough to carry on an open exchange with Mr Khruschev. In this way Kennedy avoided losing another pawn on the world chess board . . . And we have recently seen something far more promising: the Moscow Treaty banning nuclear tests other than those underground.

This is how events transpired: on June 10th, 1963, President Kennedy made a speech at American University, Washington, which was described in the United States as historic. It was a very noble speech and, I may add, of great political intelligence. This was his reply to de Gaulle's thesis: 'Some say that it is useless to speak of world peace or world law or world disarmament . . . until the leaders of the Soviet Union adopt a more enlightened attitude . . . I believe we can help them to do it. But I also believe that we must re-examine our own attitudes . . . towards the Soviet Union and towards the course of the cold war . . . No government or social system is so evil that its people must be considered to be lacking in virtue.'

These words seem to be inspired by the same spirit as the encyclical letter of Pope John XXIII, *Pacem in Terris*.

The Moscow Treaty—banning all but underground nuclear tests—concluded between the United States, Great Britain and Soviet Russia, abruptly cut short the Kennedy-de Gaulle disagreements. The reason it was concluded is because Kennedy agreed to negotiate.

It was the first step towards the end of the cold war between the allies and the Soviet Union. This stroke of moral disarmament has aggravated Communist China's hostility towards Russia and as a result opened up vast prospects for the future of the world. Here is an entirely new aspect: 700 million Chinese who are less afraid of suffering and death than the Russians and who in fifteen or twenty years will possess atomic weapons . . .

France was not present at Moscow . . . She expressed doubts, she criticised and seemingly dissociated herself from the relief felt by the rest of the world, giving the Russians the opportunity, referring to our leaders, to say to the Chinese: 'You are in very bad company.'

An official statement from the United States informed the world: 'Only three countries have not signed the Moscow Treaty—China, Albania and France.'

On October 26th, 1963, the executive Council of UNESCO adopted a resolution, by a majority of 27 votes, welcoming the Moscow Treaty, which it saw as tangible proof of the possibility of the peaceful solution of international problems, and as an important step towards the conclusion of an agreement on general and total disarmament.

France alone abstained . . .

Pretending to miss the political advantage of a reciprocal undertaking between France and the Soviet Union not to resort to force, de Gaulle wants France's seat in the conference hall, where such matters will be discussed, to continue to remain empty. 'Pointless,' he has said, 'since I, de Gaulle, have declared that France will never resort to aggression.'

Once more we see the same refusal to enter into the modern world!

Surely the strangest feature of this story is the fact that since his return to liberated France during the war, having constantly spoken of 'Europe from the Atlantic to the Urals', de Gaulle is the only person who has shown himself consistently opposed to any discussions with Khruschev.

Since these lines were written President Kennedy has been assassinated. This was the greatest misfortune which could have overtaken the free world, or in fact the world at large; for by preserving peace in 1962, he saved the Russian people as well as all the others.

On learning of this sudden and hideous tragedy, I recalled John Kennedy as I had seen him in his study at the White House—young, courageous, eager to learn all the problems of the world, full of that goodwill which is a feature of so many Americans.

Fortunately his work is being carried on by President Johnson, whom I also met at Washington, and who gave me the impression of being a strong and resolute man.

CHAPTER 5

The United
Nations flouted

THE UNITED NATIONS, WITH AMERICA AT ITS HEAD, IS WIDELY recognised as a brave attempt to bring together all people of good will, to teach them to settle their differences and to persuade them of the folly of attacking one another like wild beasts, by appealing to their reason and sense of dignity.

That great spiritual figure, John XXIII, whose interests ranged over the whole field of international politics and the welfare of mankind, paid a moving tribute in his encyclical letter *Pacem in Terris* to this great new event in world history and the hope that it held out for humanity. Of the United Nations he said, in particular: 'We consider its *universal declaration of the rights of man* to be a step towards the establishment of a judicial *cum* political organisation of the world community . . . It is our desire to see its framework and its powers applied to the extensions and fullest realisations of its purpose.

'May the time soon come when this organisation will effectively guarantee the rights which derive directly from our natural dignity and which, for this reason, are universal, inviolable and inalienable.'

The Pope concluded by issuing a call to the 'universal human family'. What high ideals! And what a contrast to the diametrically opposed stand which de Gaulle has taken. He has never tired of pouring ridicule on the United Nations, referring to it as a 'gadget'. He blames it for representing a supranational authority, capable of acting on a majority vote. He is shocked at the very idea of a supranational power. His view is that at this point the evolution of political relationships should come to a dead-end. Is it not significant that the Bishop of Verdun, speaking on August 18th, 1963, to the Christian members of Parliament should say to them: 'Our common welfare, for which you are responsible, has more than ever assumed international dimensions. The maintenance of peace depends on the harmonious cooperation of all nations.'

In times gone by France claimed to be more advanced than the Vatican!

How deeply grieved I was that de Gaulle did not make a solemn entry into the great conference hall of the United Nations in New York, followed by the representatives of our former African colonies and Madagascar, to whom we had just granted independence. If only he had said: 'I bring you France's children, and entrust them to you. Here in public debate and private conversation, these friends of ours, imbued with our culture, will be able to make a thorough study of the realities of international problems.

'I have come to tell you, in the name of France, that I vouch for their faith in your ideals and for their loyalty.' What a warm reception such an announcement would have received.

Still, it is a fact that thanks to these delegates, steeped in our culture, French is today, after English, the most frequently spoken language at the United Nations.

Between 1954 and 1961 two Americans, led by Alfred O. Haro, carried out an inquiry into the attitude of intelligent French people towards the United Nations[1]. Their conclusion was that by and large people were neither hostile nor particularly enthusiastic.

In 1956, 50% gave the view that UNO did not play an important function.

In 1959, 30% were of the opinion that its function could only be confined to that of an international meeting place.

By 1961 public opinion had changed. UNO was now held to be the most hopeful form of international community in this century.

Popular opinion, therefore, is at variance with de Gaulle's. The United Nations is widely recognised as being designed to prevent local conflicts from spreading and to aid the underdeveloped countries.

Yet that same year de Gaulle said, at a press conference on April 11th, 1961: 'France cannot see her way to adopting any other attitude towards the *united (or disunited) nations*[2] than one of extreme caution. She does not wish to participate, either with her man-power or with her money, in any of the present or future enterprises undertaken by this *organisation or disorganisation*[2].'

[1] *International Organisation*, Volume XVII, No. 1, 1963. (World Peace Foundation.)
[2] My italics.

What is the reason for this hostility? At the time when the Algerian problem was particularly pressing, de Gaulle proposed to President Eisenhower that America, Great Britain and France should settle the problem of peace in the Belgian Congo. This completely ignored the extreme sensitivity of the leaders of those nations which have been subjected to colonial rule. The very real advantages which their countries have derived from this rule have been effaced by more recent memories of subjection to remote foreign powers, boasting of their superiority; and both France and Britain were, until recently, colonial powers. Eisenhower considered this idea impractical. He was right.

What has this attitude towards the United Nations cost us? *The New York Times* of June 15th, 1963, announced that, together with the Soviet Union, France refused to accept the General Assembly's decision whereby all UNO members were to share the expenses incurred in restoring peace in the Congo and the Middle East. What was the French representative's attitude? He blamed the United Nations for trying to play the part of a government in restoring peace. But who else could play this part? He waxed indignant at the decision of the International Court of Justice, to the effect that participation in these expenses was obligatory for all members of the United Nations. What an example for France to set! This aggressive attitude particularly offended the representatives from our former colonies, now independent, who are proud of belonging to the United Nations.

At the opening of the September session of 1963, President Kennedy and Mr Gromyko were due to make speeches which, after the Moscow Treaty and the intensification of the Sino-Soviet conflict, were of paramount interest. All the Foreign Ministers of the Common Market countries, led by Germany—although she is not a member of the United Nations—were present. Only France was absent.

The American Secretary of State, the British Foreign Secretary and Mr Gromyko dined at the United Nations with U Thant. There were many subjects to discuss. The Foreign Ministers of our five Common Market partners, when dining with the American Secretary of State, must have talked about Great Britain, and about us.

France was not there—France was sulking.

During his tour of the South-east in September, 1963, de Gaulle referred to UNO as a sort of club. Just that. He denied, for example, that it had the right to intervene in order to prevent the negroes in the Belgian Congo from assassinating the whites and raping their women. Who else could be expected to intervene?

Opposition to UNO, to integration, which is the essence of NATO, to a supranational authority in Europe—in brief, to all the positive trends in world affairs—this is the distinguishing feature of the Fifth Republic. France's retrogressive influence on world affairs might well result in her being abandoned to her own disappointed dreams! It is a dismal prospect for us.

CHAPTER 6 *A coup de force to save his foreign and defence policies*

BY 1962 DE GAULLE'S FOREIGN POLICY WAS CLEARLY UNACCEPTABLE to the National Assembly, and he was well aware of this. As a result, when Prime Minister Debré, in April that year on the day after the Evian agreement which ended the Algerian war, asked him to dissolve the National Assembly—in the same way that the British Parliament can be dissolved—de Gaulle refused. This brought about Debré's resignation.

It seemed obvious that de Gaulle refused because he realised that the French were delighted that the Algerian war had come to an end; that the extreme Right, which was opposed to his Algerian policy, would be defeated; but that most of the deputies who were hostile to his European policy, despite having backed his Algerian policy, would be re-elected. This was even more predictable because the people were strongly in favour of European integration.

From then on, after the general election called for by Debré, the new Assembly could be counted on to bring down any government which failed to carry out a European policy and which agitated for a national striking force. Being unable to dissolve the Assembly, the day after its members had received a national vote of confidence, the alternative was for him to resign.

De Gaulle did not care for either of these prospects.

To make matters worse, France's political *élite*—those who are elected by their fellow citizens and who themselves elect the senators and, in accordance with the Constitution, the President of the Republic—were opposed to de Gaulle's foreign policy.

72

De Gaulle therefore considered modifying the Constitution to ensure his own re-election or that of a candidate supported by him. But to do this the new text of the Constitution had to be approved by Parliament —the National Assembly and the Senate[1]. They would not, however, approve the election of a President of the Republic by universal suffrage, which is contrary to the spirit of a parliamentary regime where power is vested in a government responsible to the Parliament and not the President of the Republic. This was the regime de Gaulle gave us in 1958. His Constitution had not been modified on this essential point.

De Gaulle thought of putting the matter to the vote of the two Chambers, but later abandoned the idea.

At a luncheon party on June 12th I met M. Debré, who assured me that the Constitution would not be changed. That evening at a dinner at the Élysée, the President of the Constitutional Council told me that he had convinced de Gaulle of the impossibility of getting it through Parliament.

On the following day, June 13th, came the *coup de théâtre*: 293 deputies came out in favour of a united Europe. The government had agreed to a debate on foreign policy but, despite the wish expressed by the Committee for Foreign Affairs, it had refused the deputies the right to express their opinion by vote, knowing that it would revolve round Europe.

The deputies reacted as follows: 280 of them signed a declaration which was read to the National Assembly by the President of the Committee for Foreign Affairs.

Here is the text of that declaration:

'We, the undersigned French deputies, having been unable to express our opinion by a vote, confirm our wish to see France commit herself to the path of European unity, which we envisage as a democratic community of nations and not as a series of conferences between governments on old-fashioned diplomatic lines.

'*We consider that the methods and principles which have proved successful in the Common Market should be developed and extended to general policies, particularly in foreign affairs and defence.*

'We propose that these should be realised in one or several stages: *the strengthening and coalescing of the various organisations of the community, the election of the European Assembly by universal suffrage, and the progressive institution of the majority vote procedure within the Council of Ministers.*

'We reaffirm our conviction that *only a United Europe, a partner on an*

[1] In September, 1962, when a third of the Senate came up for election, all the senators hostile to de Gaulle were re-elected.

equal footing with the United States, within the framework of NATO, can preserve our future liberty and peace.'[1]

There was loud applause from all the deputies except the Gaullists and the Communists. The deputies who signed the manifesto then left the hall.

This solemn declaration explicitly condemned de Gaulle's 'Europe of conferences', but was moderate in that it recommended that the reforms necessary to create Europe should be carried out in 'one or several stages'.

It bore the signatures of a large majority of the Assembly (the number of signing deputies had by that evening risen to 293—an absolute majority requires 240).

In my forthcoming survey of the Constitution, I shall make it clear that de Gaulle, undoubtedly taking advantage of the emotions aroused by the abortive attempt on his life at Le Petit Clamart[2], showed himself to be a great strategist: he did not hesitate to cross the Rubicon by vesting the people directly with the right to elect the President of the Republic by universal suffrage. He ignored the votes of the Constitutional Council and of the Council of State, which considered that he would be violating his own Constitution. The deputies whom he had dispossessed of their essential rights were thus given the choice of dishonourably submitting or of passing a vote of censure on him. The Pompidou government fell.

De Gaulle now plunged into the electoral fray, reaching out to the people by means of television appearances and exhorting his audiences to obey him under pain of seeing him return to Colombey-les-deux-Églises and abandoning them to their fate, of which he painted a lurid picture.

This is how he obtained 60% of the votes at the referendum on the election of the President of the Republic by universal suffrage, and how he then won a majority in the ensuing general election, thanks entirely to the turncoat 'Europeans'.

[1] My italics.
[2] On the outskirts of Paris.

CHAPTER 7 *January 14th, 1963—the veto against Great Britain. Could any speech have done greater harm to France?*

'De Gaulle, without being hindered by anyone, will now be able to play a lone hand in the only game he really cares for, against the United States of America, Soviet Russia and England.'

FRANÇOIS MAURIAC[1]

At the Élysée.

AT THE PRESS CONFERENCE OF JANUARY 14TH, 1963, THERE WERE 850 French and foreign journalists, photographers, film cameramen, etc.— not to mention the cabinet ministers.

A great deal of water had flowed under the bridge since the last press conference of May, 1962, which had routed the ministers who championed Europe.

De Gaulle was there on the platform, intoxicated by the flood tide of his electoral tour. He had the power. He intended to use it.

In this 'dictatorial' speech, as it was later called, he pretended first and foremost that the referendum had a bearing on the powers of the President of the Republic, although his sole concern had been *the method of his election.* He now claimed that the people had approved 'the manner in which—in the course of four years—he had discharged the duties of the President of the Republic'.

Had he violated the Constitution? The country, he said, had settled matters. Yes, just as it had settled matters by the plebiscite following the *coup d'état* of December 2nd. For this, too, was a plebiscite. 'The Constitutional reform we have carried out,' he said, (i.e. the election of the Head of State by universal suffrage) 'is in response to a truly absolute necessity in these modern times.'

An absolute necessity? Are the British, the Germans, the Scandinavians, the Italians and the Benelux countries still living in the Middle

[1] *Le Figaro Littéraire*, November 26th, 1962.

75

Ages? They do not seem to be particularly aware of this necessity, and in none of them is the Head of State elected by universal suffrage. True, it happens in the United States where there are only two parties, but Congress is master in its own domain and neither the House of Representatives nor the Senate can be dissolved. But we know only too well what the results of this form of government have been in many of the South American republics.

De Gaulle then announced that it was he who would press the button for an atomic war, which he delicately called 'instantaneously taking decisions of great consequence'. We all know what this would mean for France.

After this he condemned the 'party system'. But are there no parties in the United States, in Germany, in Great Britain and in Sweden? In what democracy are there no political parties?

As for those who did not agree with a concept which would have appealed to Mussolini, he accused them of 'exuding gall', or 'spitting bile' or of 'secreting vinegar'. How timid was this last expression!

He defined the function of a President of the Republic as follows: 'I placed by my side as Prime Minister, M. Michel Debré . . . I summoned M. Georges Pompidou and the other ministers.' According to the Constitution it was the Prime Minister alone who had the right to choose ministers. This was not the picture he had given to the Constitutional Consultative Committee of the Government which, he said, 'could no longer govern' if it was responsible to the Head of State. This theme will be developed in more detail in my survey of the Constitution.

And then came the *coup de théâtre*. The six members of the Common Market, including France, had been unanimous in agreeing to negotiate with Great Britain regarding her candidature for the Common Market. Annoyed at the slow progress of the negotiations on European policy, Belgium, the Netherlands and Italy had refused on April 17th, 1962, to continue the conversations without Great Britain. Now, with negotiations actually under way, de Gaulle decided to veto Great Britain's entry. He thought that Germany would certainly support him after his enthusiastic reception there in September, and he was not unduly worried about the complaints of the other members.

What was the reason for this veto? Because Great Britain was an island. Perhaps this detail had escaped his notice when he had accepted her candidature. De Gaulle was sceptical about her willingness to renounce 'Commonwealth preference', and this was, of course, one of the main issues that was then under discussion.

Behind Great Britain he saw the giant shadow of America. President Kennedy had reasonably urged the creation of Europe, including Great Britain. This would give the United States a partner of comparable weight with whom they could deal on an equal footing. There was no question of fusion, as de Gaulle apparently believed, nor of the entrance of the United States into the Common Market, but of a 'partnership'; in other words, an association with Europe. Kennedy had got Congress to pass a law to lower customs tariffs, which was to Europe's advantage. There was nothing to indicate that Europe—particularly if de Gaulle finally agreed to political integration—would be a weak, ineffectual partner compared with the United States. This had been proved in the 'chicken war' in 1963, a tariff dispute between the Common Market nations and the United States.

Since America had incurred enormous expenses in foreign currency to maintain her army in Germany and to support the free nations in Europe and elsewhere (expenses so vast that they even endangered the dollar, a formidable threat for the whole free world) it was natural that Europeans should respond favourably to President Kennedy's proposal, which aimed at increasing American exports, restoring the American balance of payments and safeguarding the dollar.

De Gaulle, however, was terrified by the spectre of what he calls 'a giant Atlantic community under American domination and direction'. To his way of thinking Great Britain was the melodramatic villian, ready to smuggle into the European fortress a new Trojan horse, with the American enemy in its belly.

His veto against the entry of Great Britain into the Common Market was like a slap in the face for our two great allies, Great Britain and America.

His distrust of them had been increased by the Anglo-American agreements concluded in the Bahamas. We have seen that they were the result of Great Britain's inability to bear the cost of a missile programme without American aid. So, while Great Britain and the United States were working out a military policy in which by rights we should have been participating, de Gaulle was so shocked by the Anglo-American Bahamas agreement that he declared: 'Freedom of action is a categorical imperative for a great nation since alliances have no intrinsic value. If one suddenly loses, even temporarily, one's freedom of action, there is a great risk that it will never be recovered.'

But can one imagine France fighting for her life otherwise than as a loyal ally of other nations, particularly the United States? Have not all the European countries taken shelter beneath the American 'atomic umbrella'?

De Gaulle, unfortunately, does not think so; and in support of his argument he says the one thing which could wound our American ally most. He questions her readiness to fulfil her engagements and enter the fray on Europe's side, because she could only do so with her atomic weapons i.e., by risking reprisals—a declaration which must be very welcome to the Soviets.

Concerning collaboration with our allies within the framework of NATO, he declares that our nuclear force could only 'combine its action with others, but that integration is something inconceivable in this context'. In his next breath he rejects the very idea of integration!

Only de Gaulle believes that the French nuclear force would, from its very conception, have the sinister and terrible capacity to destroy millions and millions of human beings in a matter of minutes—presumably with aircraft carrying A-bombs, opposed by rockets!

He therefore rejected the proposal made by the United States to Great Britain and France to share in a multilateral force earmarked for European defence, although the United States offered to allow us both 'to exercise free control of our nuclear capacities in the event of supreme national interest seeming to demand it'.

Such was the content of his historic press conference.

Answering questions that same day before the Council of NATO, the United States representative laid stress on the 'integrated' character of the proposed multilateral nuclear force. This caused Germany to accept the American offer in principle at the very moment that de Gaulle was rejecting it at the Élysée.

The *Frankfurter Allgemeine Zeitung* came out with these headlines: 'De Gaulle curtly rejects the American nuclear proposals'.

World reaction.

Le Figaro, next day, after giving the full text of this conference, surveyed the opinions of France's allies.

Here are some of the headlines:

America: 'Amazement in the USA'.

London: 'Resentment, but Whitehall has not given up hope'.

Rome: 'Keen disappointment'.

Brussels: 'A shower of cold water'.

There was nothing in the German papers, although Germany's reactions were just as decided; nor from Holland, who, as we shall see, was even more outspoken than Germany in her disapproval. What a harvest! Whitehall's illusions were soon shattered, and the Prime Minister led the opposition to Princess Margaret's proposed visit to Paris for a charitable cause, angered at the thought of her dining with de Gaulle, whose invitation she had already accepted.

To those journalists who asked for my views that evening, I posed the following question, which events have proved to be correct.

'Has France, in her entire history, ever dealt herself such a severe blow?'

For where are we now? France is isolated; the *Entente Cordiale*, which has saved us twice in thirty years, has been flouted; there is discord within the Atlantic Alliance; the United States is annoyed, not to say hostile towards us; the Common Market, a driving force for our expansion, is threatened with collapse—and why?

Who, in fact, forced de Gaulle to launch this attack, when it would have been so simple for him, had he wanted to oppose Great Britain's entry, to let the negotiations continue and to adhere strictly to the terms of the Rome Treaty?

To appreciate the full harm done to France by this veto, we must refer to the international press. The following quotations are relevant, for it is not enough to claim that France is isolated. We must prove it.

Great Britain: On January 15th, a correspondent of the *Monde* telegraphed: 'Resentment is general and very deep-seated in London'.

The Conservative *Daily Mail* was bitter, reminding readers that France had let Britain down in 1940 and that Britain had managed to extricate herself then. Now it had happened again.

I was so strongly reminded of 1940, that I wrote to Prime Minister Macmillan, with whom I had become friendly at a meeting of the European Council: 'The President of the Council who, in 1940, received Churchill's generous offer of a Franco-British union, which he personally accepted, wishes to express to you the affection and admiration he feels for the Great British people, our ally of two world wars.'

The Prime Minister thanked me for having written in these terms and ended with these words: 'I often remember those days during the two World Wars when the fate of our two nations depended on our common efforts.' But de Gaulle's speech did not only arouse noble sentiments. I had proof of this when, after my statement of the evening of January 14th, I received an empty envelope, with my handwritten name and address, and this simple note along the edge: 'If away try Agincourt or

Waterloo'. The comradeship of two wars, the fact that the heroism of the British nation and its leader had saved us when in the eyes of our military leaders all was irrevocably lost, meant nothing to this anonymous, brainless, heartless creature!

The *Daily Worker* wrote: 'This is the biggest slap in the face (to use the most polite analogy possible) which Mr Macmillan has yet received.'

The Observer: 'The general's two aims are that Europe should decide her own destiny and that, within Europe, France should retain absolute independence.' *Now this runs contrary not only to American and British policy but also to that of the other members of the Common Market.*

United States: Life magazine (circulation 7 million) was harsh: 'He said nothing we didn't know he had been thinking. But his manner was shockingly tactless . . . Tact has never been de Gaulle's long suit . . . there is a whiff of Bonapartism in de Gaulle's presumption to speak for a continent.'

The *New York Herald Tribune* of July 30th compares the attitude of the Fourth and Fifth Republics towards major problems: 'In America, there is only sorrow that France is no longer a partner in the great work which she did so much to launch in the days of her relative weakness— the creation of a North Atlantic community that would be the heart and dynamo of the free world.'

But de Gaulle remembers that *what France did at the period of her comparative weakness she did in spite of him.*

Belgium: The Brussels Christian Democratic paper, *La Cité*, concluded: 'Men do not change at his age.'

The Catholic *Rappel* wrote: 'Isolation which leads to a form of right-wing neutrality summed up in the ambiguous formula "Europe from the Atlantic to the Urals".'

Holland: Significantly, there was strong support in Holland for Great Britain. On January 25th the Dutch Foreign Minister, Joseph Luns, suggested that France's five partners in the Common Market should draw up a plan for a treaty between themselves and Great Britain, and that France should then be invited to accept or refuse, with all the consequences that this implied.

Italy: In Italy, on that same day, the Finance Minister, Signor La Malfa, who had proposed a 'Rome-London bridge', returned to the charge. He again called for energetic opposition to what he called the 'Paris-Bonn axis'. But his superior, Signor Fanfani, favoured more moderate and gradual action 'within a collective framework', to obtain Great Britain's entry into the Common Market.

'To follow de Gaulle would be to engender a crisis in the Atlantic world', wrote Rome's moderate *Messaggero*, which made a bitter reference to a 'restricted Europe dominated by the Franco-German alliance'.

Germany: What about the views of our largest partner in the Common Market? De Gaulle showed an astonishing misunderstanding of the reasons why his speech of January 14th should have upset the Germans. There are in fact two principles of German policy which he completely ignored:

(1) In the economic field Germany—in particular the most dynamic part of the country, the North—is orientated towards Great Britain and the United States.

(2) With regard to European defence Germany considers that the presence of the American army in her country and the integration of all allied forces within NATO are prerequisites of her freedom. This, incidentally, is equally true for France. Thus, she wants to strengthen those bonds with the United States which de Gaulle is intent upon loosening, if not breaking.

In other words, on all major problems Germany is radically opposed to de Gaulles' policy.

How can de Gaulle be ignorant of the basic premises of European policy? This is what we shall see in due course.

What happened was that these attacks on Great Britain and the United States merely aroused German feeling against ourselves.

According to Hamburg's *Die Welt*, 'De Gaulle is digging another ditch in place of the one which has just been filled,' (a reference to de Gaulle's visit to Germany which wiped out the memories of the past).

The Bonn *General Anzeiger*, also an independent paper, wrote: 'The cold refusal which de Gaulle gave again yesterday to Great Britain's entry into the Common Market can in no respect be approved by Germany.'

The Social Democrat paper, *Frankfurter Rundschau*: 'The general is true to himself . . . but whether his refusal is worthy of a politically and historically conscious statesman is another story.'

But now let us see the Bonn Government in action. On the eve of his departure with Chancellor Adenauer for Paris, where the Franco-German Treaty was to be signed, Herr Schroeder, the Foreign Minister, stated on Cologne radio that 'for political and economic reasons the entry of Great Britain into the European Community is *necessary, urgent* and in fact *very urgent*.'

On September 20th, 1963, Vice Chancellor Erhard took the opposite view to de Gaulle's with regard to the United States. In place of 'European Europe' he ventured to suggest that 'Europe is not all'. He stated that it was essential to cooperate with the United States and Great Britain, and he added that France and Germany had different ideas about defence, so there was double disagreement here.

On November 15th, 1963, Herr Hallstein, President of the Common Market Commission, stated to *Le Figaro* that the demoralisation resulting from the 'dictatorial' speech was such that 'certain members were too much inclined to take refuge behind General de Gaulle's famous press conference, in order to avoid their own commitments.'

Peking's *New China* rejoiced in these terms: 'The western world is being undermined by disagreements.'

January, 1963. The final breakdown at Brussels.

The Ministers of the six member countries of the Common Market were due to meet at the end of January in Brussels. On the previous day Signor Martino, President of the European Parliament, and former Italian Foreign Minister, publicly stated that the attitude adopted by General de Gaulle 'has cast a shadow of anxiety and distrust over Europe'. The anxiety was, in fact, very real. James Reston in the *New York Times* and Joseph Alsop in the *New York Herald Tribune* asked if, in the case of a breakdown, the United States would call on Dr Adenauer to choose between President Kennedy and General de Gaulle. Germany was to be represented at Brussels by Erhard and Shroeder, both determined champions of Britain's entry into the Common Market. They wisely insisted upon the need for restoring the unity of the Six.

Alas, the French ministers supported their leader's veto. Great Britain could not enter the Common Market against a veto by one of its members. This caused the *New York Times* to say on January 30th that the negotiations 'have ended in victory for de Gaulle and defeat for the Western world'. France was now isolated. The leading American newspaper concluded that the West's problem was to wait for the end of de Gaulle's seven-year mandate, and added: 'It is hard to believe that on this issue he speaks for a majority of the French people. France is not against the things for which the free world stands, and she is not powerful enough to create a new world in Charles de Gaulle's image.'

The Chancellor and his Foreign Minister came to Paris for the signing of the Franco-German Treaty, but in what a strained international atmosphere! The Chancellor felt bound to write a letter to President

Kennedy in which he stressed the strictly formal nature of this treaty, and stated that there was no question either of the Federal Republic's loyalty to NATO or his own agreement in principle with the mutilateral Atlantic force proposed by Kennedy and rejected by de Gaulle.

The opinion of the leaders of the Common Market Commission.

What did these leaders think of the veto against Great Britain? No one was better qualified than they to judge whether negotiations between Great Britain and the Six had been doomed to failure as de Gaulle claimed, or whether on the contrary they still had a chance of success, at the time de Gaulle issued his veto.

The following declaration was made on February 5th, before the European Parliament at Strasbourg, by the eminent President of the Commission, Professor Hallstein (Germany) in his usual restrained words: 'It is impossible to consider that negotiations had practically fallen through when they were interrupted, or to say that it was obvious that they could never succeed.' This flatly contradicted de Gaulle.

He concluded: 'The truth is rather that they were going through a difficult phase which called for certain important concessions on Britain's part, but there was a reasonable chance of agreement being reached.'

The Vice-President, Mijnheer Mansholt (Holland), a specialist in agricultural matters, and who supports our policy in this sphere, was far more forthright: 'It is false to say that the negotiations had reached an *impasse*. The reason for the failure must be sought in the desire of a single man to return to the system of old-fashioned coalitions and his ambition to create a third power between the East and West. Before any further progress can be made in the European Community (Common Market) a choice must be made between the wishes of the Five who would permit Great Britain's entry provided she accepts the Treaty of Rome and the temptation of playing a game of see-saw in a coalition dominated by one nation.' (*Le Figaro*)

On June 5th, 1963, the European Community presented its private report to the European Parliament. On the subject of de Gaulle's veto the report pointed out that from January 1st, 1966, such a situation could no longer arise because decisions then would be taken by a majority vote. In the meantime it recommended that contacts be resumed between the Community and Great Britain, although France was more than reticent on this point.

A deadlock had, therefore, been reached.

After the Brussels breakdown.

The London *Times* wrote on February 1st: 'President de Gaulle has made it plain that the game he is playing is not the same as that being played by the friends and allies of France.'

On February 2nd, the *New York Times* wrote: 'It sounds fantastic, but it's true. What Premier Khruschev could not do with all his dire threats of atomic annihilation has been done for him by . . . President de Gaulle of France. In vetoing Britain's entry into the European Economic Community and in refusing full French military cooperation with the North Atlantic Alliance, de Gaulle has dealt a body blow to both European and Atlantic unity . . . President de Gaulle may delay it (Atlantic partnership) but cannot thwart it. The past cannot veto the future.'

'Vetoing the future'—that was the concensus of world opinion, as a result of France's delaying tactics on Europe, her refusal to integrate into NATO, her condemnation of the United Nations, and her veto against Great Britain, and, by implication, America.

De Gaulle knew that once Britain entered the Common Market, the Brussels Commission, British language and British influence would be paramount, instead of French as at present. We agree with him that this would be unfortunate, but it is foolish to try to erect a barrier against a powerful current, because one day the dam will be swept away, with disastrous results.

Under the title 'Europe *vs.* de Gaulle', the *New York Times* of February 5th wrote: 'His attempt to dominate Europe has been denounced by, among others, Premier Fanfani as a "menace", Prime Minister Macmillan as "folly as well as ingratitude", Belgium Foreign Minister Spaak as "monstrous", and by Dutch Foreign Minister Luns as "authoritarian and dangerous".'

At the same time the relationship between de Gaulle and Macmillan deteriorated, with the British Prime Minister disputing de Gaulle's version of the conversations they had had at Rambouillet.

On February 2nd, Vice-Chancellor Erhard announced to the *Suddeutsche Zeitung* that he was in favour of Franco-German unity, but added: 'I do not know if hopes are improved by the fact that at regular intervals we tackle problems *on which we know that we can never convince the French President and on which there can be no basic agreement*.' He also observed that 'one hardly dares to ask what the slogan "From the Atlantic to the Urals" means.'

After all, Germany lies between the Atlantic and the Urals!

The same day Dutch schoolboys voted that courses in French should be suspended, by way of reprisal, and about 100 German students also demonstrated against French policy.

France alone . . .

On February 8th, the headlines in *Le Figaro* read: 'Adenauer in the Bundestag: "De Gaulle promised me to consider Great Britain's entry into the Common Market . . . *as soon as the Franco-German Treaty came into force*".'

It is in force and Great Britain is still outside the Common Market.

On March 29th, the European Parliament, with the exception of the French UNR deputies, voted unanimously in favour of Great Britain's entry into the Common Market.

On April 2nd, Stewart Alsop, quoting Walter Lippman, wrote in the *Saturday Evening Post*: 'De Gaulle has "struck a blow at the foundations" of American defence and foreign policy. In fact, he has struck not one blow but several.'

Such were the results of the disastrous press conference of January 14th, 1963. Was I wrong to ask whether any speech had ever done so much harm to France?

The Directory of three.

This was another of General de Gaulle's dreams. Since we are considering Europe it is worth making a reference to this unfortunate proposal.

In September 1958, four months after his return to power, de Gaulle's first diplomatic action resulted in a setback which increased his bitterness towards the United States. This was his suggestion to set up a Directory of three—America, France and Great Britain, to run the affairs of the free world.

Up to that point there had been a recognised situation; the British were privileged allies by reason of their common origin and language, and also the courageous behaviour of their people during the war. To accept de Gaulle's request would have been to transform a *de facto* into a *de jure* situation, with France as an additional participant. But this would have left Germany and Italy outside. Eisenhower refused, and de Gaulle reverted to his original way of thinking, which was not greatly to America's liking.

CHAPTER 8

The Franco-German Treaty and its disappointments

THIS WAS THE OUTCOME OF ONE OF THE TWO GOALS AIMED AT BY THAT great statesman, Adenauer. To be accurate, the way to Franco-German reconciliation had been paved by Robert Schuman's ECSC, and this was the first step towards Adenauer's second goal—the creation of Europe.

The Chancellor, however, was in favour of a treaty because of its symbolic character. This aroused anxiety and some bitterness in the minds of the Italians, who had not even been informed, and the members of the Benelux countries, who were afraid that Common Market problems might be settled over their heads by straight agreement between these two powerful partners. The sound but modest Franco-German agreements envisaged mutual consultations between ministers and high officials of the two nations in addition to military contacts.

The preamble demanded by the German Parliament.

The Germans foresaw the danger of seeming to give solid support to Gaullist policy, and, in fact, Italy and the Benelux countries had no real reason to be alarmed. For Germany disagrees with de Gaulle on all major issues. Therefore, despite the fraternal embrace at the Élysée on the day the treaty was signed, when it was due for ratification by the Bonn Parliament it became obvious that Germany would refuse to sign unless a 'preamble' were included so as to make it clear that signature of the treaty did not necessarily imply agreement with de Gaulle's policies. De Gaulle protested in vain against this preamble, particularly to the

Mayor of West Berlin when he visited Paris. But the preamble was unanimously voted by the Bundestag.

Here then is a summary of the two conflicting policies:

The German view (as contained in the preamble)	*De Gaulle's attitude*
The preservation and consolidation of agreements between the free nations.	He antagonised the most important of them in his press conference of January 14th, 1963.
. . . with a particularly close collaboration between Europe and the United States.	In his view the United States is the enemy of 'European Europe'.
The unification of Europe.	He is opposed to this, and is only prepared to accept occasional discussions between leaders, who could only make decisions unanimously.
. . . including Great Britain.	He had just vetoed Great Britain's entry into the Common Market.
The consolidation of the existing European Communities.	He is opposed to them and makes no secret of his contempt for their 'technocrats'.
To abolish tariffs by negotations between the Common Market, Great Britain and the United States.	On January 14th, 1963, he announced his opposition to President Kennedy's offer to Europe of an economic association.

The German deputies voted unanimously for the foregoing proposals and proceeded to ratify the treaty. When it came up for debate in the French Chamber, most deputies deliberately ignored the flagrant differences of opinion. But this did not do away with them.

Press views on the preamble.

Germany: The Social Democratic *Neue Zeitung* of Essen wrote on May 17th: 'It was not the preamble alone which prevented the German

87

Federal Republic from being harnessed to the triumphal chariot of de Gaulle's nationalistic European policy. It was the actions of the government and the opposition with a view to tightening still further our bonds with the United States, despite the pact concluded with Paris.'

Belgium: Paul Struye, in the Catholic paper *Livre Belgique* of May 20th, stated: 'The event has already shown that on several burning questions the Governments of Paris and Bonn have, since signing the treaty, been obliged to take opposite points of view.' And he recalled that Paul-Henri Spaak had declared that this treaty was 'a bad thing'.

Switzerland: The Liberal *Gazette de Lausanne* of May 17th: 'The Germans are trying to forge the closest links with the United States. They still rely upon the Americans to ensure their liberty.'

This of course is good sense. Were France one day to be so stupid as to invite Germany to choose between the United States and herself, Germany would undoubtedly choose the United States. For Germany is not mad.

On May 14th, the *Institute of Social Sciences* took a poll in West Germany as to the relative popularity of various foreign statesmen. The results gave Mr Kennedy 70% of the votes, Mr Khruschev 7%, General de Gaulle 5%. The last-named would have headed the poll the day after his visit to Germany the previous September . . .

As for the USSR, they sent us a note accusing France of having 'created a bloc with forces in Germany deeply concerned in preventing the development of Franco-Soviet relations', whereas 'friendly relations between Paris and Moscow could have developed into the bond between Eastern and Western Europe'. The note also condemned the treaty as 'giving off an odour of gunpowder and military hospitals'.

Ratification by the French Chamber

This took place on June 14th, 1963. Since the Constitution did not allow any preamble to be added to the Franco-German Treaty, as the German Parliament had done, the Treaty was ratified by the French National Assembly by 325 votes only.

The independent *Die Welt* asserted on June 15th: 'In future we must devote ourselves with increased energy to the work of unifying Europe.'

But it takes two people to make a marriage . . .

The independent *Deutsche Zeitung* said on June 14th: 'The way in which the reconciliation of France and Germany has taken place has aroused the mistrust of our European partners. The loudly trumpeted friendship between France and Germany has apparently lost its value from one day to the next.'

Germany rejects an agreement on grain prices.

Immediately after the ratification of the Franco-German treaty, Germany, in Geneva, was urging her Common Market partners to accept the American system of a mutual reduction of tariffs between the United States and the Common Market. Yet in the meantime in Brussels, Herr Schwartz (the German Minister for Agriculture), alone of his five colleagues, refused to lower German grain prices, a worse blow to France than to any other member of the Common Market. According to our previous agreements, German agricultural prices were to be lowered to come more into line with French prices, so as to arrive at an average price.

'Useless,' said the German minister ironically. 'The steadily rising cost of living in your country will bring up your grain prices to the German level!'[1]

'This is a violation by Germany of her undertaking of January 14th, 1963,' said the Minister for Agriculture—the very day of the historic press conference which was to strain our relations with both the Old World and the New.

Whereas Germany boasts a liberal policy of exchanges with third parties, here she was in favour of maintaining high agricultural prices exactly where the shoe pinched most. In this debate, however, we were supported by the formidable Herr Mansholt, the architect of European agricultural policy.

But that day Germany said 'no'.

The lesson to be drawn from the failure of the first Franco-German conference.

At the beginning of July, 1963, at Bonn, General de Gaulle and several of his ministers met Chancellor Adenauer, future Chancellor Erhard and their ministers.

Two questions were on the agenda:

The French were seeking German support at the meeting of Ministers of the Common Market for an agricultural settlement, which was vital in view of France's need to export her surplus agricultural produce.

[1] In 1962 the French cost of living index was twice that of Germany.

For their part the Germans, anxious for de Gaulle to reverse his veto of January 14th against Great Britain, insisted that in the meantime France should agree to the closest possible relations between Great Britain and the Common Market.

There was total failure on both sides, and added humiliation for us since it was decided to approach the Brussels 'technocrats' to try to find a solution which would satisfy the Germans.

In order not to come back empty-handed from this escapade, arrangements were made for mutual exchanges of students.

After this General de Gaulle left the Schaunburg Palace together with Prime Minister Pompidou, Foreign Minister Couve de Murville, Minister of Armed Forces Messmer, Minister of Agriculture Pisani, Minister of Finance Giscard d'Estaing, Minister of National Education Fouchet, and Secretary of State for Youth and Sport Herzog.

Would de Gaulle realise that his European formula for occasional meetings of heads of states or government, accompanied by their ministers and advisers armed with documents, was doomed to failure?

This pathetic Bonn Conference proved that the intervention of a third party was necessary. This third party was the Commission composed of European technicians, disregarding their own nationalities, knowing that by serving Europe they would be serving their own country.

We have seen that the treaty did nothing to diminish the basic disagreements between French and German policy, and that it also disturbed our other partners of the Common Market.

To crown everything, it increased the tension in our relationship with those nations whose rockets could in a few minutes wipe France off the face of the earth.

CHAPTER 9

The Moscow Treaty:
China and de Gaulle

Ten months after Cuba.

IT WAS NOT SO LONG AGO, WHEN THE RUSSIANS EXPLODED THEIR gigantic bombs and American submarines armed with Polaris missiles arrived in the Mediterranean, that the Soviet press announced that in the event of war the penalty for France would be that 'famous cities on the shores of the Mediterranean would be reduced to the state of Pompeii'.

Barely ten months had elapsed since the discovery of the launching sites in Cuba installed by the Russians, which nearly caused a nuclear holocaust.

For years the Russians and the allies had intermittently discussed the problem of disarmament at Geneva.

And now in Moscow, on August 5th, 1963, Mr Khruschev, together with the representatives of the United States and Great Britain, signed a treaty banning the most dangerous of nuclear tests from the point of view of fall-out—tests in the atmosphere and under water. Only sub-terranean tests are still permitted. This agreement is designed to prevent the spread of nuclear weapons and represents a step forward on the path to disarmament.

In fact, both sides announced that this treaty was only a beginning, and that there was now a prospect of a non-aggression pact between the countries of the Warsaw Pact and those of NATO.

This did not, however, prevent Mr Khruschev, on his way to Berlin, from giving a few small pinpricks to the West. We must not forget that in the eyes of his rivals he is the leader of the 'appeasers'.

The moral and political importance of this agreement was recognised throughout the world.

The Secretary General of the UN, U Thant, declared: 'The present agreement constitutes an important step towards the reduction of international tension and the strengthening of peace.'

M. Paul-Henri Spaak, the Belgian Foreign Secretary, declared: 'The Moscow tripartite pact is not so important for its technical arrangements, but it constitutes the first step towards a general change of attitude to disarmament.'

Svenska Dagbladet of Stockholm: 'It would obviously be an exaggeration to say that this treaty constitutes a turning point in the history of the world, but it represents the first ray of hope in the darkness which has shrouded the nuclear question for nearly twenty years.'

The *Gazette de Lausanne* of August 6th considered that the Moscow treaty was 'the first concrete result recorded since the beginning of the interminable discussions on disarmament.'

Al Allhbar of Cairo wrote: 'The treaty constitutes a constructive stage in the reduction of tension and the cold war.'

Hopes rose high throughout the world. A hundred countries were to support the Moscow Treaty.

China, France and Albania alone refused to do so.

Why China?

Even before the treaty was signed, China had protested vehemently. 'It's a swindle,' wrote the Chinese press. 'In the guise of a bogus disarmament, it is really a transaction directed against ourselves. The Russians have betrayed the cause of Socialism by associating themselves with the American imperialists. They agreed in October, 1957, to give us the secrets of the atom bomb. In 1959 they broke their word. And now in order to keep us disarmed, while they themselves are armed to the teeth, they are trying to forbid us carrying out the nuclear tests which they have often made and on such a large scale!'

On December 3rd, 1963, at the World Council for Peace held in Warsaw, a Chinese delegate protested against the wording of the final resolution including praise for the Moscow treaty which, he maintained, must be condemned as 'an American-Anglo-Russian conspiracy'.

It is obvious that China intends to play her part as Communist leader of the coloured races—the underprivileged nations against the nation protected by the proud white race—Russia included. They do not intend to be excluded from the race for nuclear power, particularly since they have an Alsace-Lorraine in the shape of Formosa.

Malinowski, the Soviet Minister for Defence, replying to the Chinese protest, said that the attitude of the Chinese 'amounts to virtual complicity with those who seek a thermo-nuclear war and are opposed to a peaceful solution of international problems'.

And here is the main accusation: 'The Chinese leaders are openly hostile to a combined world Communist movement and to all the peace-loving peoples of Europe, Asia, Africa and America. They are stirring up international tension.'

Rude Pravo of Prague, which invariably follows the Moscow line, wrote on August 1st: 'The Chinese Government sees as its main goal, not disarmament, but the creation of its own nuclear weapons . . . Why does China want this? Have nuclear weapons been necessary thus far to safeguard the Chinese revolution? Is the power of the Soviet Union not sufficient guarantee for the Chinese people against an attack by the imperialists? There is only one answer. The Chinese leaders want to have their own nuclear weapons to carry out their expansionist policies.'

The conclusion of this article makes one think of the reply given by a Chinese minister to Marshal Tito, who had expressed his horror at the idea of a nuclear war: 'Well, even if it destroyed 300 million Chinese there would be 300 million left.'

This contempt for death and suffering, which is one of the characteristics of the Chinese people, will be one of the major factors in world politics before the end of the century.

And now France.

De Gaulle gave his opinion at his press conference of July 29th, 1963: 'The fact that the Russians and the Anglo-Saxons have decided immediately to cease their nuclear tests in the atmosphere and under water is in itself satisfactory.' He then went on to minimise the importance of the decisions by pointing out that it was not the first time that nuclear tests have been interrupted; but he did not appear to be struck by the fact that this time it was by virtue of a treaty.

Putting our American ally and our Soviet adversary in the same category, he added: 'It must be stated that the treaty does nothing to change the threat represented by the nuclear weapons of the two rivals against the world and, above all, against nations who do not possess them.'

Once more he declared that 'if one day the Americans and the Russians . . . agree to the supervised destruction and banning of their nuclear weapons, we ourselves will renounce our possession of them with the best will in the world.'

De Gaulle announced that before the end of 1963 he would suggest to the three nuclear powers certain plans for disarmament. This he does not appear to have done.

He ended by asserting that France would not allow herself to be side-tracked from her determination to possess a nuclear force.

With regard to America, de Gaulle maintained that what happened at Moscow showed that 'the path followed by United States policy does not conflict with ours'.

The Times observed: 'There is no reason why President de Gaulle's expected aloofness should hold up the process tentatively begun last week in Moscow.'

The *New York Times* on July 30th, 1963: 'President de Gaulle himself foresees the possibility of a future understanding with the Soviets, but his present negative and obstructive stand will certainly not speed the day. The contradictions in de Gaulle's policy are further emphasised by his strategic concepts. He would base Western strategy on American nuclear power and France's position. But he proposes to destroy all nuclear stockpiles and delivery vehicles, a plan that would also destroy the West's nuclear deterrent that assures peace.'

This is why Americans are right to call upon their European allies—particularly the French and the British—to create conventional forces.

Federal Germany signed the Moscow treaty. De Gaulle did not, therefore, speak in the name of Europe.

In her isolation, France, which used to be so responsive to modern trends and ideas, appears to be unaware of the wind blowing from Moscow which has restored the hopes of so many nations.

CHAPTER 10   *Kennedy pledges*
the United States

WEST GERMANY, WEST BERLIN, HIS ANCESTRAL IRELAND, ENGLAND, Milan, Rome and Naples—this was President Kennedy's itinerary from June 23rd to July 2nd, 1963. He was acclaimed everywhere, particularly in Frankfurt, West Berlin and Naples.

It was at Frankfurt on June 25th that he made his historic speech in which he said proudly: 'The firmness of American will, and the effectiveness of American strength, have been shown in support of free men and free governments. In Asia, in Africa, in the Americas, and above all, here in Europe we have undertaken and sustained, in honour, relations of mutual trust and obligation with more than forty allies. We are proud of this record which more than answers doubts.'

The President renewed his country's pledge at Frankfurt in these moving words: '. . . war in Europe, as we learned twice in forty years, destroys peace in America. A threat to the freedom of Europe is a threat to the freedom of America. This is why no administration in Washington can fail to respond to such a threat—not merely from goodwill but from necessity. And that is why *we look forward to a united Europe—in an Atlantic Partnership*[1]—an entity of interdependent parts, sharing equally both burdens and decisions, and linked together in the task of defence as well as the arts of peace . . .

'That defence . . . is indivisible. *The United States will risk its cities to defend yours*[1] because we need your freedom to protect ours.

'Your nation is in the front line of defence—and your divisions, side

[1] My italics.

by side with our own, are a source of strength to us all.

'*These conventional forces are essential*[1], and they are backed by the sanction of thousands of the most modern weapons here on European soil and thousands more, only minutes away in posts around the world.'

The following remarks were addressed to the Russians: 'Together our nations have developed for the forward defence of free Europe a deterrent far surpassing the present or prospective force of any hostile power.'

Kennedy added that it was necessary to create a genuine *European deterrent*[1] force closely united to the Atlantic deterrent. 'Such a force would bring strength instead of weakness, cohesion instead of division. It would belong to all members, not one, with all participating on a basis of full equality. And as Europe moves towards unity, its role and responsibility, here as elsewhere, would and must increase accordingly . . . European officers from NATO are being assigned to Strategic Air Command Headquarters in Omaha, Nebraska.'

United Europe and cooperation instead of division—what a lesson!

The press on Kennedy's European visit.

United States: From Washington the correspondent of *Le Monde*, Alain Clement, wrote: 'By contradicting General de Gaulle, Mr Kennedy is sure of the unanimous support of American public opinion,' and: 'Franco-German relations which have already been seriously impaired, have now reached a stage of open enmity.'

The *New York Times* of July 1st considered that the policy proclaimed by Kennedy was exposed to two dangers—on the one hand the Communist challenge, and on the other, the nationalism of President de Gaulle.

Kennedy answered this by emphasising once more the doctrines of interdependence and indivisibility of defence.

Germany: The *Frankfurter Allgemeine Zeitung* of June 29th wrote: 'It would be a grave error of judgement on the part of the French to suspect the United States and the German Federal Republic of intending to isolate France . . . If anyone is isolating himself it is General de Gaulle.'

Great Britain: The *Sunday Times* of June 30th wrote: 'The President's speeches have also shown that Washington's view of General de Gaulle's competing policy for France and Europe is that it is a temporary block on the road, not a fundamental and enduring diversion.'

[1] My italics.

CHAPTER 11

July 29*th,* 1963 — *de Gaulle*
attacks America

AT A PRESS CONFERENCE AT THE ÉLYSEE, WITH ALL THE USUAL
ceremony, de Gaulle decided to retaliate against the press for their
worldwide attacks on him after January 14th. For these had continued,
despite all official reassurances to the contrary.

With Great Britain, in his view, *hors de combat,* de Gaulle switched his
attack to America: 'There has been considerable excitement, particularly in American newspapers, for some months.' And he spoke
tauntingly of American 'spasms on the part of what is called opinion.'
This is how he treated the all-powerful public opinion of the greatest
democracy in the world. After this he said he found 'that the tone and
the tune with regard to France are somewhat extreme.' He seemed to be
quite unaware of the consequences of his press conference of January
14th. In contrast to the picture he painted of the prosperity of France
which, in his opinion, was obviously fortunate to possess a good political
regime, he spoke of 'a certain tension which exists over there [in the
United States] and which is caused by pressing troubles both at home
and abroad, and also to the uncertainties caused by frequent disturb-
ances.' A delicate allusion to the painful colour bar problem.

After this he enumerated his personal quarrels in the past with the
United States: the Yalta Conference, his refusal to meet Roosevelt, the
problem of our zone of occupation, and then the famous plan for the
European Defence Community which he was proud to have helped to
thwart. He had no reason to be proud of this, for the EDC solved the
problem of the use of nuclear weapons by German soldiers serving with
the European army. Russia had retained such a fear of the German
army that if the latter were now to be given nuclear weapons we should

D

be brought to the brink of war. Today, de Gaulle's feud with the United States centres around the organisation of Europe, NATO, our nuclear force, and the United Nations—in fact, on all the problems that matter.

After a brief reference to the 'moral capital' of his past[1], de Gaulle declared that between Paris and Washington there was 'political divergence' and 'journalistic ill will'. One would have liked to see him give a list of the former and to propose solutions rather than to hear him add fuel to tensions which already exist. Hearing him speak with such detachment and levity, one wonders whether he realises that our very existence as a free people depends on our American ally.

There followed a bitter diatribe against a 'so-called supranational Europe in which France would have vanished, except to pay out and air her views, a Europe which would have been run by anonymous technocratic committees, a Europe, as a result, without political reality, without economic resources, incapable of defending herself and destined . . . to be merely a satellite of that great power . . . the United States of America.' And it was *he* who spoke, in one of his press conferences, of 'grumbling' and 'bad temper' on the part of his opponents.

The arrow had been loosed. The opponent was still America just as in those long-distant days when he arrived in Paris proclaiming his dream of 'Gibraltar to the Urals'.

Proudly de Gaulle informed the Americans that they were too late. 'Since those days France's position has changed profoundly. She is prosperous and has access to the means of power,' i.e. the nuclear weapon. 'She has dispelled the storm clouds which hindered the building of Europe (sic).'

So it is de Gaulle who wants to create Europe! 'A Europe which must be European,' he specifies, for the benefit of the Americans. A Europe left to her own devices. He should try saying that to Chancellor Erhard: he would be very popular. For 54 million Germans are behind Erhard on this vital point, as on many others.

We are back to the slogan of 'France in the forefront'. For de Gaulle never develops and never can develop because his policies are based on purely sentimental foundations.

It is worth noting, in passing, that in the economic field de Gaulle seems quite oblivious to the considerable achievements of the 'technocrats' on the Commission of the Common Market in Brussels.

With regard to the hopeful prospects born of the Moscow Treaty,

[1] A reference to his solution of the Algerian problem.

France has her own ideas on the subject which, he says, will one day be revealed. We have seen how France refused to associate herself with the UNESCO resolution approving the treaty and offering its cooperation.

De Gaulle rejects in advance the projected non-agression pact between East and West, denouncing it as pointless. Why? Because he does not wish to deal with the countries of the Warsaw Pact 'under the Kremlin yoke'. He will not admit that it is with one's enemies that one has to make peace. France will never attack, he says, therefore her signature is valueless. He has spoken, and that is enough. How is it he cannot see the benefit deriving from any step designed to relax tension, remembering that, only a short time ago, nuclear war nearly resulted from the Russian installation of rocket sites in Cuba?

What is the American guarantee worth? That would depend on whether the leaders would run the risk of extermination by using their nuclear bombs against Russia. And de Gaulle said this a month after Kennedy's solemn pledge at Frankfurt: 'The United States will risk its cities to defend yours.' The American President hoped that the past record of his country would 'more than answer doubts'. Apparently it did not.

Moreover, de Gaulle, just as if he brought to NATO the twelve German or the six American divisions, instead of a mere two with a few heavy tanks, demanded 'important modifications' regarding France's participation in the alliance. Categorically rejecting integration, which is the life-source of NATO, he hurled this poisoned barb at America: 'Their balance of payments and dollar problems are their chief worries.' Such worries for America would also be worries for the free world, which would be affected by a fall in the dollar; but this interdependence seems irrelevant to de Gaulle.

Once more he stressed that there were differences between the two countries concerning 'certain international problems'. He did not, of course put a name to these difficulties, nor did he offer any solution. He seemed quite content with this strained atmosphere.

To sum up his opinion: 'While in the past everything attracted us to the Americans, nowadays everything divides us.' Nor is there any ray of hope since he has nothing constructive to suggest. How arrogantly he laid down his conditions, not with a view to coming to an arrangement but simply for the sake of talking . . . and with little hope of success. First, America must '*make up her mind about this new situation* and when she has done this *then* it will *doubtless*[1] be necessary to coordinate our

[1] My italics.

respective policies, as far as it is possible, and in every situation as it occurs.' Doubtless—but it's not all that certain.

America has to go on her knees first!

One can imagine how annoyed the average American must have been to read this haughty summons on the part of an ally who had just with-drawn her last warship from NATO command.

A further summons was addressed to Germany, who had opposed France's request to settle the agricultural question. The ministers of the six nations in the Common Market were given until December 31st, 1963. Either the matter has to be settled by that date or the Common Market would disappear, said de Gaulle. He could hardly have been serious, for in three years' time he will not be able to use his veto to block decisions, for they will be taken by a majority vote.

I sincerely hope that this settlement will come about, but the chances of success would have been far greater if, in exchange for the sacrifice which he asked the Germans to make on agricultural prices, de Gaulle had agreed to create the integrated Europe which Germany, whose land and capital have been cut in two, desires.

As for the conversations between the 'Anglo-Saxons' and Khruschev, he says: 'What happened at Moscow shows that the course followed by United States policy does not conflict with our own.' On which point? Silence. Is de Gaulle really opposed to an easing of tension, despite the great hopes aroused by the Moscow Treaty? Yet again he says: 'For the moment France will not associate herself with any scheme arranged over her head concerning Europe or Germany in particular.'

This, however, did not prevent Germany from sending her Foreign Minister, Herr Schroeder, to ask the British Government's support in denying implications that the Moscow Treaty constituted a *de facto* recognition of Communist East Germany.

This press conference of July 29th did not create the same furor as the earlier one, when de Gaulle pronounced his veto against Great Britain's entry into the Common Market. On the other hand, it widened the gulf which, since then, has separated France from the United States and her other Allies.

'American patience is exhausted . . . This is the last straw.' These, according to *Le Monde* of August 1st, were the official comments heard two nights previously in Washington.

De Gaulle's demand for an agricultural agreement to be reached before December 31st, 1963, was conveyed to the German delegation gathered in Brussels for the Council of the Six. It was pointed out that the President of the French Republic had in mind a kind of agricultural autarchy in Europe, which was by no means foreseen by the Rome Treaty. It was wrong because an undertaking had been given on January 14th.

To sum up: De Gaulle has satisfied his grudge against the American press which, since his veto of January 14th, has pointed a finger at this European who has refused to cooperate on any plane—either military or economic. It is France who will have to pay the price of this press conference as she did after January 14th.

CHAPTER 12   *France alone in a*
hostile world

FRANCE ON HER OWN—ALONE INDEED!

I intend to show, through quotations from the world press, the extent of the moral and political damage caused by the press conference of July 29th, 1963.

Radio Moscow that night declared that 'this speech has emphasised the depth of Franco-American differences'.

Pravda announced that de Gaulle has 'joined the ranks of the madmen', and the Soviet press accused de Gaulle of speaking in 'cold war tones' and protested against 'the slanderous accusation made against the Soviet Union'.

Certainly de Gaulle had performed quite a feat, not only by antagonising both the Western world and the Soviet Union, but also by incurring the displeasure of the uncommitted nations.

So much for the other side. What about our own?

We have seen that the United States underlined the fact that the three countries refusing to sign the Moscow Treaty were China, Albania and France.

Sir Alex Douglas Home, the present Prime Minister of Great Britain, then Foreign Secretary, made four points in a television appearance on July 29th.

(1) The French attitude did not in any way invalidate the value of this agreement—welcome news for British views, who after de Gaulle's recent insulting behaviour must have been relieved to note that, on this major international issue, France was ignored.

(2) Exchange of views between the three powers—still the United

States, the USSR and Great Britain—would take place on ways of preventing the spread of nuclear weapons.

(3) The conversations would deal with measures tending to prevent surprise attacks. 'Now for the first time,' said Home, 'Mr Khruschev has said he'd have observers in Russia . . .'

(4) Home implied that the signing of a non-aggression pact between NATO and the Warsaw Pact was unlikely.

The world press is again unanimous after July 29th.

United States: Since America was de Gaulle's main target it is worth looking first at public reactions there.

Raymond Cartier, who cannot be accused of lukewarmness towards de Gaulle, telegraphed from New York to *Match* (August 24th, 1963) on the general feeling of the 'American giant' with respect to France.

'The order of the day here is a concentrated attack on France. The indictment of de Gaulle has become the main topic of conversation around town. Gaullist France is accused of having disrupted Western unity. She is reminded that after all she is a second-class power whose means do not measure up to her pretensions. Nor is she indispensable. A league comprising America, Great Britain and Germany, supported by all the other European countries from Norway to Greece, could revive the great plan for an Atlantic community which was shattered by General de Gaulle's conference last January. Isolated in the economic, military and political fields, France, in her artificial majesty, would be put in quarantine *until the day General de Gaulle disappeared from the public scene.*[1] She would then be re-admitted into the Western community after being humiliated in punishment for her presumption. Recent German developments, the imminent coming to power of Erhard, strengthen the chances of putting such a policy into action.'

Raymond Cartier had the courage to end as follows: 'The interruption of the progress towards Europe, the only worthwhile political objective of our age, may perhaps have proved fatal to the whole enterprise.'

Raymond Cartier's analysis was later shared by Dean Acheson, former Secretary of State and adviser to President Kennedy, who was sent to speak to de Gaulle on Kennedy's behalf. On November 19th, 1963, Acheson declared that it was of the greatest importance that the governments of the United States and of Federal Germany should plan their

[1] My italics.

strategy and their policies together. This collaboration is in force today.

The *New York Times* of July 30th considered that de Gaulle 'has made little contribution to progress by his latest pronunciamento', and thought it urgent that he should go and speak seriously to Washington.

Regarding the doubts expressed by de Gaulle concerning American pledges to Europe, *Le Figaro* of August 1st recalled President Kennedy's further statement at Frankfurt: 'Those who would doubt our pledge or deny this indivisibility [of Europe and America]—those who would separate Europe from America or split one ally from another—would only give aid and comfort to the men who make themselves our adversaries and welcome any Western disarray'. An obvious allusion to de Gaulle.

Great Britain: Referring to de Gaulle's proposal for a four-power conference on disarmament, the Liberal *Guardian* wrote that such a meeting would have no satisfactory result and that Russia and America would be far more likely to negotiate directly, leaving out both Britain and France, than to set up a Council of Four to which countries with more or less well-founded claims to a nuclear device might presently demand admittance'.

The Times thought that 'had France not boycotted the disarmament committee she could have had the invitation'.

Africa: The *Ghanaian Times* of Accra on July 30th voiced the feelings of the uncommitted nations: 'We are astonished at France's aggressive attitude on a matter so vital to the survival of the human race . . . The only result will be to isolate France from her allies and from world opinion in general.'

Le Peuple of Algiers wrote on the same day in the same vein: 'The French President has just publicly defied world opinion, completely misinterpreting the true significance of the Moscow Treaty.'

Holland: The Catholic *Volkstraat* of the Hague wrote that day: 'It becomes more and more evident that General de Gaulle's conception of Europe and a European community is basically different from that of the founders of European unity.'

Sweden: Dagnes Nyhater, the Stockholm Liberal newspaper, wrote, also on the same day: 'De Gaulle is playing the role of the injured party because the great powers have made an arrangement with the Kremlin without even asking France to join in—as if he himself for two years had not systematically sabotaged every effort made at Geneva to work out a treaty banning all nuclear tests.' For there is general agreement on the need to prevent the spreading of nuclear weapons.

Switzerland: The Liberal *Journal de Genève* wrote on the following day: 'It should be noted that since he came to power, General de Gaulle has worked hard to withdraw the French forces from NATO. Of course, should a crisis arise, cooperation would be restored, but the character of the alliance has changed. Some reforms may be necessary. What is regrettable, however, is that General de Gaulle confines himself to criticism instead of indicating the modifications which seem to him indispensable.'

They are not merely modifications, alas. If war broke out he wants France to defend herself 'in her own fashion'.

After President Kennedy had answered de Gaulle on this point (that integration is essential) without actually mentioning his name, *Le Monde* noted on August 3rd: 'Today, as yesterday, agreement between the United States and France depends upon the acceptance by General de Gaulle of the integration of Western defence. This detested word was obviously used by President Kennedy intentionally. But the Head of State has shown more obstinately than ever his total opposition to integration, because it runs counter to his ideas of national sovereignty and his own role. The split between Paris and Washington has never been so deep.

Germany: Hamburg's *Die Welt* wrote on July 30th: 'As on January 14th, General de Gaulle yesterday uttered a double "no"—"no" to the Moscow Treaty because France is not prepared to sacrifice her nuclear weapons, and "no" to a non-aggression pact which could build a bridge between NATO and the Eastern bloc . . . In January the harshness of tone opened up a chasm between France and her allies. This time there was no commotion.'

The *General Anzeiger*, a Conservative Bonn paper, wrote on July 30th: 'After General de Gaulle's latest pronouncements France finds herself even more isolated . . . We should be careful in Bonn not to fall into step with General de Gaulle.'

Here now are some facts which speak for themselves. Federal Germany agreed to sign the Moscow Treaty despite her fear that the allied signature to the treaty might be considered as an implicit recognition of Communist East Germany.

Another important item of news: Federal Germany agreed to build tanks jointly with the United States, at a time when France was under the impression that Germany had accepted her own light tank.

The law which governs German policy—agreement with the United States—has thus been applied in both these cases.

Le Monde, too, could not help asking if the Franco-German treaty had any meaning since, to say the least, the Bonn and Paris views on diplomatic and military matters were in no way concerted.

Roger Massip, for his part, observed in *Le Figaro* that one would have to be a super-optimist to claim that Federal Germany's support of the Moscow Treaty represented a success for French diplomacy. Questioned by the press, our minister stated: 'Our relations with Germany are at odds.'

Alas, since then, on September 27th, 1963, de Gaulle has announced that France does not want the protection of the United States.

This is where France stands after five years of Gaullist policy.

To put it plainly—it is isolation, not the 'splendid isolation' of Victorian England, but isolation as a result of antagonising some and defying all.

CHAPTER 13 *September, 1963—de Gaulle takes a hand in the Vietnam crisis*

IN 1954, AFTER FRANCE'S DISASTROUS DEFEAT AT DIEN BIEN PHU, A conference was held at Geneva. Vietnam was divided into two military zones, and it was decided to hold elections to decide the political future of the Vietnamese nation.

The elections never took place. The military frontier became a political frontier splitting Vietnam in two—communist North Vietnam with its capital in Hanoi, and anti-communist South Vietnam with its capital in Saigon.

Communism was solidly entrenched in North Vietnam.

China and North Vietnam gave effective aid to the South Vietnam communists, at war with the Saigon government.

America, playing her part as defender of the free world in Vietnam as in Korea, gave military and financial support to this government. Her participation has already cost her 210 men killed[1] and a million and a half dollars a day.

The South Vietnam government was led by a Catholic, Ngo Dinh Diem. Only one-tenth of the population are Catholics. I had tried to dissuade him from accepting power, and his failure to follow my advice finally cost him his life. He had been much criticised in America for some time. The appalling suicides of the Buddhist monks, transforming themselves into living torches, had finally aroused American public feeling against him. The American government, anxious and distressed, made vigorous representations to the head of the Saigon government.

[1] This figure covers the period from January 1st, 1961, to April 6th, 1964, and includes battle and non-battle deaths.

107

So grave was the situation that the United States decided to send a distinguished ambassador, Mr Henry Cabot Lodge, to Saigon. It was then that de Gaulle released to the press the text of a declaration he had just read to the Council of Ministers. It stated that France recognised the role that the peoples of the two Vietnams could play 'provided they were allowed to carry on their activities *independently of external interference*, in peace and internal unity and in harmony with their neighbours.' He concluded: 'Every national effort that is made in Vietnam to this end will find France ready, as far as she is capable, to bring about a friendly measure of cooperation with this country.' From a military viewpoint, the position was serious.

So it was that, in the midst of this serious situation, France, who had left Indo-China many years ago, intervened and offered assistance to the peoples of Vietnam if this would serve to make her independent of foreigners—in other words, of the United States. The solution did not apply to North Vietnam, which will probably never shake off the Communist yoke.

Nicolas Chatelain sent a telegram to *Le Figaro* in which he described as follows the effect on American opinion caused by de Gaulle's unexpected interference in the Vietnam crisis:

'Washington, September 2nd. We have so often said on other occasions that de Gaulle has reached new heights of unpopularity in America, that we find it somewhat embarrassing to repeat it. And yet the comments made here by newspapers, television speakers and political cartoonists, are not merely critical. This time they are really vicious towards him. A typical cartoon shows a disabled de Gaulle swathed in bandages and plaster, hailing an abashed Uncle Sam across the ocean with the cry: "Hi, you over there! Take the advice of an expert."

'Newspaper comment is more specific: France, which in Indo-China only managed to get herself defeated at Dien Bien Phu, who has on her conscience long years of colonial exploitation, the bombing of Haiphong and Hanoi, etc., who washed her hands of Vietnam at the time of the Geneva agreements, is really ill-advised to come forward now to tender advice. What has the USA done in Saigon for eight years if not to try to fill the gap created by the French default? America's task is not an easy one, but it is not the business of a "bankrupt" to teach a lesson to those who try to hold on to something which he has been only too eager to let go.[1]

---

[1] It should be pointed out, in fairness to de Gaulle, that he only came to power four years after Dien Bien Phu.

'This is how de Gaulle's pronouncements have been generally interpreted for the public. Nor has the press failed to remind readers that the General recently made ironical allusions to the difficulties of the dollar. Is de Gaulle going to exaggerate our troubles whenever they occur?'

Our papers informed us that our ambassador, M. Hervé Alphand, had again visited the State Department to explain that General de Gaulle did not mean what he said, that his declaration was 'a long-term one' and not 'directly bound up with the present situation', that it was 'more political than military'.

After this, one has to rack one's brain to fathom de Gaulle's pattern of thinking. Perhaps he imagined, for example, that Khruschev, happy to have the chance to score against Mao Tse-tung, would urge the Hanoi government to give its support to this touching Vietnamese reconciliation under a neutral flag.

This, of course, ignores the fact that North Vietnam is Communist, that its leader Ho-Chi-minh is a Communist, and that the country has a common frontier with Communist China for thousands of miles. Even if she wished to abandon Communism for neutrality, there is nothing to prove that her powerful neighbour, who incidentally helped her to win the battle of Dien Bien Phu, would allow it, so that any attempt by Moscow in this direction would be unthinkable.

As for South Vietnam, if she were rash enough to declare her neutrality, after thanking the Americans for services rendered, she would topple into the Communist camp.

It is worth adding that the *New York Times* revealed on September 5th that the French diplomatic service—it quoted names—had played a significantly anti-American role in Saigon since President de Gaulle had dragged France into the crisis.

Paris was supposed to have extended the mission of our ambassador in Saigon, with orders to obstruct Mr Cabot Lodge, who was considered in Paris, quite wrongly, to be anti-French. The French ambassador was accused of having intrigued with his German and Italian colleagues.

It was natural that de Gaulle's indiscretion should be criticised by both friendly and hostile newspapers.

In its usual sober tones Boston's *Christian Science Monitor* wrote on September 3rd: 'Few would quarrel with such an attempt—provided its aims and effects were not harmful to the West as a whole.'

The *New York Times* considered that following France's refusal to sign the treaty partially banning nuclear tests, and her opposition to negotiations with the Soviet Union and participation in the NATO nuclear force, President de Gaulle's declaration on Vietnam was calculated merely to weaken the position of the United States within the Western alliance.

The Washington *Evening Star*: 'The imperious general apparently would water down, if not eliminate entirely, America's role in Vietnam. This is the same thing, of course, that he has been attempting to do in free Europe . . . '

The *New York Post*: 'President de Gaulle is again demonstrating his formidable flair for antagonising the US . . . It is obvious that de Gaulle is deliberately equating America's anti-Communist commitments in South Vietnam with Soviet and Red Chinese support of North Vietnam.'

The *New York Sunday News* stated that in Washington's view the net effect of de Gaulle's declaration was to further complicate both Washington-Paris and Washington-Saigon relations.

The London *Sunday Times* expressed the following opinion: 'General de Gaulle's personal intervention can only be interpreted as support for the Ngo family against the United States. Although the French President's statement is wrapped in his usual elevated ambiguity, it can do nothing but make the situation worse.'

The *Journal de Genève*: 'General de Gaulle's remarks have been welcomed in America like the comments of a back seat driver when the gears have been crashed.'

La Suisse: 'The gap between France and the United States is gradually widening and the Atlantic alliance will soon be no more than an illusion, a dangerous illusion.'

Le Libre Belgique: 'The United States are in a difficult position in Saigon . . . General de Gaulle has seized this opportunity to make a declaration whose effect is still being discussed.'

The *New York World Telegram*: 'As soon as Khruschev quietens down, de Gaulle tunes up. Now he has stuck his nose into the embarrassing mess in South Vietnam. He has offered to cooperate with that unfortunate country, in throwing off "exterior influences", obviously meaning the US as well as the Communists.'

The Sydney Daily Telegraph: 'Whatever the reason for it, de Gaulle's statement is no good for Western solidarity and is liable to do more mischief than good in South Vietnam.'

As for President Kennedy, on September 3rd, in a television interview, he displayed great self-control and even courtesy towards a Head of State who had played such a part in history and who was so much older than he. Kennedy pointed out that de Gaulle was a friend and that everything he said must be listened to. He went on to assert that to leave Vietnam would be a grave error, and people who saw him on television tell me that he added with a smile: 'We should like to receive a little more cooperation, real cooperation.'[1]

On September 12th, 1963, *La Nation*, the paper of the UNR, told us how we should interpret the reactions caused by de Gaulle's interference in American policy: 'These are obviously errors or a lack of vision on the part of the American leaders, who sometimes arouse General de Gaulle's irony, and certainly not of the great, friendly nation with whom France would like to work more along common lines of thought.'

How sorry we should feel for those leaders who are 'lacking in vision', with which we are so generously endowed.

As for the irony, may it be spared our successors in Indo China!

Let us now take a look at the overall picture in Asia.

The shadow of China, with its enormous population, reaches out even farther over the whole of South-east Asia, waiting to envelop it entirely.

Preferring, as he said, a 'cool revolution to a hot revolution', with which he believed his country to be threatened, Prince Sihanouk, the Cambodian Head of State, convened a congress, attended by several thousand people, which decided to dismiss the American military mission. He then summoned the Chinese officials and solemnly announced that he had made his son his successor at the head of his own political party. This son is finishing his studies . . . in China.

This is the sort of difficulty which the Americans have had to face in trying to save South Vietnam from Communism. Surely this policy deserved something better than an invitation, discreet as it was, from de Gaulle to the people of South Vietnam to get rid of those who have sacrificed both men and money in an effort to preserve their freedom.

And now, a new development: after Diem's execution the army has seized power in South Vietnam.

France refuses to recognise the new government, to show that she disagrees with Washington on this point as on all others.

General Duong Van Minh, President of the Revolutionary Committee and Head of State, said, regarding de Gaulle's stand: 'To be neutral you have to be strong, and we are not yet strong enough.' This is good sense.

How could South Vietnam, at war with the Communists, possibly negotiate a neutrality pact with North Vietnam, when the departure

[1] *Le Figaro*, September 4th, 1963.

111

of the Americans would obviously result in a Communist victory? This would indeed be putting her head in the wolf's jaws.

There has been no French ambassador in Saigon since September, 1963, and no recognition of the new government. Are these the best ways of defending French interests in South Vietnam?

Regarding the refusal to recognise the new government on the grounds that it is pointless, the foreign correspondent of *Le Figaro* telegraphed: 'This attitude has been keenly criticised both by the generals and in American circles. They interpret it as a criticism of the programme announced by the Junta, the main point of which is an intensification of the war against the Viet Cong.'

The protest by the South Vietnam students.

Another piece of late news: On December 20th, 1963, several thousand students from Saigon University and the higher classes of the schools, carrying banners bearing de Gaulle's name and rude comments, staged a mass demonstration through the city. They marched to the French Embassy and the French Cultural Centre, shouting 'Neutrality is treason' and other anti-French slogans.

Thus the untimely intervention by de Gaulle in the affairs of South Vietnam did harm not only to the South Vietnamese, the Americans and the defence of South-east Asia against Communism, but also to France, whose prestige in that part of the world had until then been high.

This is the danger of impulsive actions based on faulty information—a real danger in a regime such as ours. It would be unthinkable in a parliamentary regime.

To complete the picture let us add to this sequence of pin-pricks de Gaulle's greetings to Albania, which supports China in her opposition to the Soviet Union, and which, with China and France, refused to adhere to the Moscow Treaty.

After a second anti-French demonstration by Vietnamese students, a meeting of high-ranking officials passed a resolution which urged the breaking off of diplomatic relations with France.

The result of this unfortunate interference is that whereas French popularity in Vietnam used to be greater than American, today France is accused of wanting, in fact, to hand over the country to the Communists.

CHAPTER 14

September, 1963—de Gaulle refuses American protection and takes the offensive

AFTER THE WORLD REACTION TO HIS TWO SENSATIONAL PRESS conferences of January 14th and July 29th, de Gaulle considered it prudent, on his 'South-eastern tour', to clear up certain discrepancies. In the speeches he made in the provincial town squares, UNO was no longer a 'gadget' but a 'useful forum' to which, however, all action was forbidden because it would play the part of a 'super-state'. The Atlantic alliance was 'wholly necessary'. He congratulated himself on the Moscow treaty. He spoke in a good-natured tone and referred to himself as an 'old fellow'.

But he could not escape from his basic conflict with the American giant, which, as we have seen, had begun before he even came to power. His irritation mounted to such a peak that, in spite of his general mood of conciliation, he was actually more outspoken than ever. At Belley, in the Ain, on September 28th, he gave vent to this cry: 'We do not want the giant of the West to lead us, *not even* to protect us.' At Bourg-en-Bresse he again refused this protection.

So having said 'We are allies,' he rebelled openly against the conditions necessary for the efficient working of this alliance; this, in fact, is what he has always done and this has naturally caused great anxiety within the alliance. Yet he had never dared to say that he rejected a form of protection which he knows to be vital for his country. Of all his outbursts, this one was the most sensational.

Against the organisation of the defence of Europe, in which America is predominant, de Gaulle uttered this shout of protest: 'France must be France in relation to all countries, however great they may be . . .

In these organisations the question for us is to know whether we are going to merge with them; that is to say if we are to accompany such and such a foreign country—we know full well which—or if we are to remain France. Well, we shall remain France!'

I do not think that these chauvinistic remarks would have aroused any enthusiasm in the anonymous writer who reminded me that Agincourt was on the Somme and Waterloo in Beligum. What I find humiliating is not the fact of having an ally more powerful than oneself, but benefiting from an alliance while refusing it the collaboration it required. And this, alas, is precisely our case. But even if the French press did not challenge his remarks, they were the subject of strong comment elsewhere.

The *New York Times* of September 30th wrote: 'President de Gaulle has chosen this hour of world hope to issue a new declaration of "independence" that goes beyond his previous pronouncements. He proclaims that France will not only conduct nuclear tests but will pursue an independent course in international affairs; independent, in particular of the "Anglo-Saxons".'

The *New York Post* wrote on the same day: 'It is ironic that the President of France . . . should be urging a go-it-alone policy the same week that the President of the United States was telling his people that this country, for all its power, could not afford to play a lone hand in world affairs.'

NATO and the Mayor of West Berlin answer de Gaulle.

Although these words did not come as a surprise to most members of NATO, they did arouse in many people the kind of feelings which were expressed in West Berlin at a great meeting held on October 22nd, 1963, at the Rathaus. This was the occasion of an international symposium on 'The European Community within the Atlantic framework'.

Discussion of the French attitude was on the agenda, but France declined the invitation to be officially represented. We have arrived at the point where our arguments can no longer be defended in public outside France.

Mr Stikker, Secretary General of NATO, the successor to Paul-Henri Spaak, declared that NATO could only exist under the nuclear shield of the United States and that *its existence and its future* depended upon cooperation between Europe and North America.

Herr Willy Brandt, the dynamic mayor of West Berlin, then took the chair. If there is a man for whom European defence has dramatic and immediate meaning it is he, whose frail skiff is tossed by the waves of the surrounding Communist sea. Here, according to the *New York Herald Tribune* on the following day, are some of his statements. Of de Gaulle he remarked: 'We honour the great but we must not let them intimidate us.'

He welcomed the reconciliation of France and Western Germany, but declared that it could not be an end in itself, the cornerstone of a policy. He said that the only alternative Europe had to being a partner of the United States was not being a third force but an unimportant collection of small national obstinacies.

The Atlantic partnership and the process of European unification was of equal importance. 'One must not wait for the other.'

He regretted that the unification of Europe had been on ice for almost a year. He is moderate. 'The shining optimism of yesterday has been dulled . . . a poisoned breath lies over Europe.' So much for the press conferences of January and July.

But he added: 'The will of the peoples for European unity can easily be reawakened. The nations of Europe want to see action.'

With reference to France's rejection of Britain's bid to join the Common Market, Herr Brandt declared that it was necessary to get rid of out-of-date and damaging national feelings.

When one thinks of the importance of Willy Brandt in Germany and the importance of Germany in Europe, these words give food for thought.

At Valence during his South-eastern tour, de Gaulle said: 'There are certain people who seem terrified by France's independent attitude. They call it isolation. It is nothing of the sort. Never has France been so sought after as she is today.'

He went on to give examples, asserting: 'It is not only those poor countries cut in two or in three by the clash of foreign interventions [shades of Vietnam!] who feel that the free arbitration of France could hold out a chance for their unity and in consequence for their peace.'

And our ministers insisted before the French deputies: France is not isolated.

Here is the extreme result of trying to give practical application to the unrealistic dogma of 'France in the forefront'—France blaming America for protecting her, even embarrassing the Americans who are saving our face in Vietnam.

If America continues to protect Europe it is in spite of de Gaulle's personal attitude.

Many people are surprised at her lasting patience. It is because

America's pledge has been given to others who believe in it. And it is also because the collapse of Europe would be an unspeakable catastrophe for America.

De Gaulle proclaimed his independence in military matters after having told NATO: 'We reject, for our part, the organisation of any system which would take away from us the freedom of action of our forces and our responsibility for our defence.' As if there were any other way for the nations of Europe to defend themselves against the Soviet peril than by linking themselves together, placing themselves under collective discipline, and integrating their forces in NATO, with the American army here in Europe and disposing of an atomic fire power at present superior to that of the Soviets.

On the following September 30th, at Lyons, de Gaulle launched an even fiercer attack on an *integrated Europe*: 'We demand that they [our partners] create it on the basis of the existing states and not by annihilating themselves in some sort of integration, which would merely deliver up to *one or other* of the two foreign hegemonies, a soulless, spineless and rootless Europe . . . '

So here we have our American allies placed on the same footing as the possible future Soviet adversary! By the same token, they are foreigners, while every day of liberty that we enjoy is a debt to the Americans! In the history of universal ingratitude, it would surely be France that would take the prize if she were to follow him in this.

Up to this point he had merely been airing one of the oldest of his grievances. But now he found a new means to feed it. France was to offer 'an example and comfort' to the underdeveloped nations. He knew that America, one of the two world powers, had her difficulties in South-east Asia and in Latin America. He had just made his intervention in Vietnam. He was on the point of visiting Latin America. He. knew that he would be demonstratively welcomed, both for his own sake and also as a form of protest against something. Thanks to her independence, he said, 'France offers every sort of nation an example and comfort . . . ' What a lead these words give to the impulses of any nations in Latin America at present in the throes of evolving a national personality! To countries divided in two or three—Vietnam for example—where the exterior intervention of the United States and China come face to face, 'France, mistress of her own soul, has something to offer which will sustain their courage and good sense.' We have seen for ourselves that it doesn't work, either in France or Vietnam!

It is not without anxiety that one anticipates the grievances which will be given an airing by his tours of South America. The Americans felt the same. Indeed, when de Gaulle arrived in Mexico, ex-president Truman said: 'If he pokes his nose into our affairs, we shall cut if off for him.' De Gaulle was wise enough to show caution.

In support of this policy, the services tell us that: 'It was interest and not the wish to save us that brought the Americans into the war. They would not have come in at all had it not been for Pearl Harbor.' Yet we know that if the American people had not been a people of spirit and could have contented themselves with settling accounts with the Japanese in the Pacific, we would still today be subjects of the Nazi empire. Such wreckers of Franco-American friendship as these have probably not visited one of the great American War Cemeteries in France or Luxembourg, where so many young men have been laid to rest because theirs is a great nation with an ideal in its heart.

CHAPTER 15   *The 'lobster war' and*
the Bizerta base

THE STORY OF THIS COMIC-OPERA WAR AND ITS DISASTROUS
consequences throws some light on the working of such a regime as ours.

Certain groups of French fishermen, who had been operating very
profitably off the Mauretanian coast, had the idea of extending their
activities to the other side of the Atlantic. They settled on a spot off the
coast of Brazil, south of Bahia, where lobsters are found on submerged
ledges at depths of 250–650 ft. They sent their ocean-going trawlers to
take soundings for fishing.

The maritime conference held at Geneva in 1958, attended by France,
had ruled that the sea-bed and ledges belonged to the coastal state. The
Americans had insisted upon this clause because these ledges could be
used by submarines.

France's case was that lobsters were not covered by the Geneva conference. The United States and Latin American countries challenged
this view and boarded the French vessels. An agreement signed between
France and Brazil stipulated that in the event of litigation the Hague
court should arbitrate.

In the spring of 1963 France brought an action against Brazil before
the Hague Court and invited her to state her case. The Brazilians
refused to appear, which was a point in our favour. It was in fact an
important economic problem. Brazilian factories on the coast, financed
by Brazilian and American capital, export twenty million dollars worth
of canned lobster to the United States. The canners were enraged by
the arrival of the French trawlers and urged their authorities to take a
firm stand.

For two years, while negotiations were in progress to try to find some basis for agreement, Brazil tolerated one or two French vessels. A profit-sharing scheme was proposed by the trawler owners, and was accepted by the French government provided that the principles of fishing rights were not affected. Brazil was also prepared to compromise, but proposed limiting the number of French vessels allowed to fish.

Negotiations dragged on.

Finally, the trawler owners requested General de Gaulle personally to ensure the protection of their vessels by sending gunboats; they then despatched five fishing vessels, which were boarded by the Brazilian navy. The French gunboats did not intervene. The French ambassador in Brazil visited the Brazilian President and informed him of the disagreement.

'I do not want any trouble with France,' replied the President. 'I am therefore giving orders to release the boats and I authorise them to fish for three days along the coast.'

But fifteen days were needed to fill the holds of the French ships with live lobsters. Consequently, they continued fishing after the three days' grace had expired.

The Brazilian newspapers roused public opinion. The President of the association of French fishermen demanded that the French ambassador should call for the intervention of a destroyer, the *Tartu*, which now appeared on the scene.

Tempers were running high in Brazil. It was now the eve of the carnival. The Brazilian Minister of the Navy ordered a cruiser and an aircraft carrier to meet the *Tartu*.

In the streets of Rio de Janeiro the incident formed the main theme of the carnival. Masked revellers were disguised as lobsters. It was a national event. A great parade was staged to coincide with the sailing of the Brazilian cruiser and aircraft carrier sent to search for the *Tartu*. War pay was granted to the crews of these two ships. This brought protests from the Brazilian crews which had remained ashore. Since they were at war they, too, should be given war pay! They were given it.

The *Tartu* returned to France—a somewhat inglorious incident for the French Navy.

De Gaulle sent for the Brazil file. He discovered that Brazil's outstanding debts to France were considerable, and recalled our ambassador, M. Bayens.

On August 17th, Brazil, with a view to ending this conflict, decided to send her finest diplomat, Sr. Vasco da Cunha, as ambassador to Paris. He was a personal friend of General de Gaulle and had met him during the Algerian war. He requested to be allowed to present his credentials in Paris. There was no reply. Days and weeks passed. The Brazilian Press, incensed, announced: 'We are being humiliated. Let us withdraw our request for his acceptance.' The Brazilian government played for time, still hoping that consent would be given, but finally withdrew its request.

It is true that the Brazilians have repaid their debt at a slower rate since France turned a cold shoulder. On the other hand, we have three important interests in Brazil: iron smelting, textiles and chemical products, and France has invested more than a thousand million francs in that country. Even so, Brazil is having economic troubles. The fall in the price of raw materials, in other words of her principal resources, has hit her hard. Unlike the French colonies, she has no guaranteed outlet for her products.

The problem is serious because in the contest of South American politics Brazil is the keystone of a very fragile structure, which is liable to collapse under the pressure of serious events. The north-eastern states, which have for some years been suffering from drought, are already showing those symptoms of unrest which create fertile ground for Communism.

What is more, the structure of Brazil's internal economy demands attention. The country is badly organised. Apart from Itamarti, her Quai d'Orsay[1], inherited from the Portuguese, her administration is inefficient. She has neither tax inspectors nor anything similar to our National School of Administration. So it is extremely difficult to put any political programme into operation.

Finally the traditional friendship between France and Brazil is by nature deep-seated and sentimental, which makes it very precious to us. This is one good reason for practising a policy of tolerance towards this great country.

But de Gaulle refused to yield.

Ministers who knew the position—there were several of them—and the President of the Committee for Foreign Affairs of the National Assembly, Maurice Schuman, called upon de Gaulle and informed him that the situation was deteriorating. In vain. De Gaulle considered the majesty of France had been outraged.

Had he been living under a parliamentary regime the consent would have been given and friendly relations restored. But we live under the government of a single man.

[1] The French Foreign Office.

The vital base of Bizerta is evacuated.

In 1961 France refused to hand over the Bizerta base to Tunisia. The Tunisian President, apparently for domestic political ends, attacked this base—a hopeless offensive which was repulsed, unfortunately with very heavy losses. Our Tunisian compatriots, who had already suffered greatly, were the object of reprisals which caused further misery.

On September 5th, 1961, at a press conference, the French President explained with his usual clarity and forcefulness the reasons for our refusal to abandon Bizerta.

'I suggest that you study the map,' he said. 'Then you will see that Bizerta occupies an exceptional position at a spot where the Mediterranean narrows into two basins, an eastern and a western.

'The countries which border the second, in other words the western, are under a threat of aggression coming from the other part—that is to say from the east. They must bear this possibility in mind as long as the world situation is continually dominated by the prospect of a war launched by the East against the West.

'And then you should look at the position of France on the map. France, in the case of an enemy invasion of these waters, would be vitally concerned, militarily and politically, in events which took place in those coastal areas adjacent to her territory, and who would inevitably be directly implicated in the defence of both shores of the Mediterranean.

'So when one has considered these facts, it can be understood that France will not and cannot, under existing conditions, expose herself, expose Europe and expose the free world to the possibility of Bizerta being captured by enemy forces.'

Since then the international situation has improved as a result of the conversations between the Americans and the British with Mr Khruschev, although neither East nor West have expressed any readiness to reduce their military strengths in the slightest.

The reasons for retaining Bizerta are still valid; but an official communiqué merely stated that with modern weapons—another reference to our striking force?—the base had become useless.

Has national pride been salved merely because the Commander-in-Chief of the Mediterranean fleet announced that an evacuation had never been effected so quickly? Perhaps it is because under the present regime public opinion has become so blunted that apart from a question put to the Senate by Édouard Bonnefous, the evacuation of Bizerta produced no reaction whatsoever.

121

CHAPTER 16   *December 23rd, 1963—*
              the 'stateless men' of
              Brussels save Europe

IT WAS A GREAT DAY AND A GREAT LESSON.

We have seen that on January 14th, 1963, de Gaulle, intoxicated by the electoral successes of the previous November, launched his veto against Great Britain. Several of our partners in the Common Market, faced with his refusal to create Europe, then declared that in these circumstances they would wait for Great Britain's entry into the Common Market before re-discussing Europe. So Great Britain was not the only country involved.

On July 29th, de Gaulle widened the gulf which separated France from her partners by attacking the United States.

The resentment among the members of the Common Market against de Gaulle's 'dictates' was so general that despite the pledges they had given on that day—January 14th—there was some doubt as to whether they would now agree to settle the agricultural problem so vital to France. On July 29th, de Gaulle, sensing this danger, threatened to break the Common Market unless the matter were settled before December 31st.

De Gaulle's threat undoubtedly helped to bring about a quick decision, and on December 23rd, Mm. Couve de Murville and Pisani stated our case brilliantly; but failure would have been certain had not the members of the Common Market Commission—the 'technocrats', 'Eurocrats' and 'stateless persons'—saved the situation, thanks to their imagination, their authority and their devotion to the cause of Europe. Particularly worthy of mention was the decisive intervention of its President, Herr Hallstein, and the courage with which one of the Vice-

122

Presidents, Mijnheer Mansholt, spoke against the views of the government of his own country, Holland.

Had they not won the day, and had de Gaulle carried out his threat and broken the Common Market, can he have imagined what would have happened?

Germany and Great Britain, followed by our partners of the Common Market, would certainly have formed a new community which would have lost no time in negotiating an agreement with the United States, whereas France . . .

Alluding to the press conference of January 14th, 1963, the German Foreign Minister, Herr Schroeder, declared: 'The Common Market has recovered from the blow it received at the beginning of the year.'

The London *Times* said the same thing in almost identical words. World opinion was unanimous as to the importance of this event.

During these dramatic sessions in Brussels the ministers of the Six acted as litigants, and the members of the Commission as judges and peacemakers.

Here is an example of Europe in action!

From 1959 to 1964 official France no more understood the problem of the unification of Europe than official France between 1932 and 1938 understood devaluation.

Will de Gaulle ever understand that a Frenchman, or a German or an Italian who has become a European, is a more highly developed individual and also a better Frenchman, a better German, a better Italian?

One thing is quite certain: Europe will eventually triumph.

But why has so much time been lost?

Let us learn the lesson of that day, December 23rd, in Brussels. Let us elect a European Parliament by universal suffrage, which would duly elect a President of the United States of Europe. This Parliament would control the policies of the European Economic Community, which would have full authority in foreign affairs and defence.

Above all, let us not return to the futile 'occasional discussions' of the Fouchet plan, with its national officials.

We must refuse to paint an imitation window on the wall of Europe!

123

CHAPTER 17   *A new attempt at*
                European integration

DE GAULLE, AS SKILFUL A TACTICIAN AS HE IS A STRATEGIST, SENSING
that the French support of the idea of Europe and that the victory of
the 'technocrats' has dealt a decisive blow to his doctrine, realises that
it is no longer enough to pay lip-service to Europe in his speeches. He
has to hold out some hope of a new development. To a question put by
journalists at the Élysée on January 2nd, 1964, he replied: 'At the
moment the climate seems to be favourable for making headway over
Europe. People seem to want it to make progress. It is a question of
knowing how to do it, at what time and to what extent. It needed an
initiative. We have made suggestions and others can do likewise or
follow up our own.[1]

What goodwill towards Europe!

But the problem is not as simple as he maintains. Two conditions
have to be fulfilled. Before uniting we have to ask ourselves whether we
agree on a common course of action. Now we know that on all the main
problems (integration into NATO, the strategy of NATO and relations
with the United States, Great Britain's admission into the Common
Market, President Kennedy's 'partnership') de Gaulle totally disagrees
with our five partners of the Common Market. The first step is to reach
an agreement with them on these problems, which will be easy enough
once the French people open their eyes to realities.

When that day dawns the second problem will arise: the form which
European union will take. Here, too, de Gaulle is in total disagreement
with our partners.

[1] *Le Monde*, January 4th, 1964.

124

In his press conference of March 15th, 1962, de Gaulle pointed out that our partners want the integration of the Six into Europe, whereas France—'his France'—supports the idea of simple cooperation.

On July 29th, 1963, de Gaulle spoke from the heart. He began with a flood of hatred against 'a so-called supranational Europe in which France would have disappeared except to pay out and air her views' and followed this with a tirade against the 'technocrats' without whom Europe would have been doomed in December, 1963.

Is there a single one of our partners today who would be content with occasional talks on 'simple cooperation'—discussions at which each delegate would arrive with his files to defend his national interests, with no one to give a casting vote? Would there be one voice in favour of such a powerless Europe?

For the solution of this problem we must also wait for France to put her own house in order.

January 14th, 1964. Great Britain wishes to take part in the negotiations: Belgium and Holland favour a postponement.

As if to mark the anniversary of de Gaulle's veto, Great Britain informed all the members of the Common Market—except France—of her desire to take part right from the start in the negotiations on European political unity.

On the same day Belgium's Foreign Minister, M. Spaak, stated that he had never had any difficulty in reconciling his loyalty to Europe with his loyalty to the Atlantic Alliance. After firing this arrow at Gaullist foreign policy, he underlined the serious disadvantages of the existing standstill on political unification. He repeated that an 'integrated Europe is the only valid ideal' and he informed de Gaulle: 'Nothing will be done in the near future, before the British General Election, for before any progress can be made we must know what kind of European policy the next British Government will have.' And underlining France's isolation he warned us: 'A certain number of the countries of the Six attach major importance to this problem.'

But will the next British Government accept an integrated Europe, 'the only valid ideal'? Alas, no! De Gaulle, as we have seen, has made the fate of a political integrated Europe depend upon the convenience of Great Britain.

The intervention of Mijnheer Luns, Foreign Minister of Holland, a country which has always supported an integration of the Six, shows the extent of the damage caused by our attitude towards the European problem. He stated: 'I much prefer a more indefinite kind of political integration, *including the greatest possible number of countries*, to an enforced integration which would be limited to the Six.' And he concluded: 'Personally I am of the opinion that we should explore certain possibilities [among the Six] and then negotiate with Great Britain and the other European countries.'

This was utter confusion.

Mijnheer Luns also put forward this practical suggestion: 'The Six must at least be in agreement among themselves on foreign policy before new institutions are created. At the moment they are not.' And he gave as examples European defence and President Kennedy's 'Atlantic partnership'.

By disagreeing with everyone on everything, France today has made any new attempt to create an integrated Europe impossible—and, I repeat, it will not be possible until the eyes of her people are opened to realities.[1]

I am still hopeful that the damage is not irreparable.

---

[1] The only reform which might be carried out *since, according to M. Pompidou, France's opposition to it had weakened,* is the merging of European executive bodies. This would involve the amalgamation into a single Ministerial Council of ECSC, EEC and Euratom.

CHAPTER 18   *A Directory of three:*
Germany, Great Britain
and the United States

WHEN ROBERT SCHUMAN LAID THE FOUNDATION STONE OF EUROPE, NO
one was under any doubt that France would assume the leadership.

There was no question of it being Germany, who had unleashed on
Europe two calamitous world wars, and who, in the second, had been
responsible for such appalling atrocities.

Yet while de Gaulle disagrees on *all* problems with *all* our partners of
the Common Market, it is Germany who is now in agreement with *all*
of them on *all* issues.

This caused the famous British historian, Arnold Toynbee, to compare de Gaulle with those who once 'worked for the King of Prussia
unintentionally'.

The only chance of political greatness offered to France in modern
times was the 'great man' who promptly threw it away. He wanted
France to be the leader in Europe but he did not want Europe! Will
history ever forgive him? And if war broke out one day, would it ever
forgive France for having refused, out of vainglory, to contribute to a
common allied defence effort?

The fundamental disagreements which existed between France and
Germany, as between France and the other members of the Common
Market, came out into the open as soon as Ludwig Erhard, Dr Adenauer's successor, defined his government's policy in Bonn, in London
and in the United States.

On the need to integrate national forces into NATO and the impossibility of any European country privately undertaking its own defence, he said: 'NATO assumes a particular importance in seeking a solution of these problems [of defence], *for today there is no national, entirely independent, military force capable of defending its country effectively. Defence has become a common task.*' He does not reject integration with NATO or talk about making war 'in one's own fashion'.

On this basic problem, as on all the others, the Chancellor expressed the feelings of all the members of the Common Market, with the sole exception of France.

During the crucial debate on agriculture in Brussels in December, 1963, we saw Germany refuse—despite the pledge given at Brussels eleven months previously to our Minister for Agriculture—to discuss the agricultural programme, so vital for France, unless the European Community undertook to adopt the Kennedy plan, which de Gaulle had condemned as a threat to European independence. De Gaulle had to give way.

Mr Butler's first visit as British Foreign Secretary was to Chancellor Erhard at Bonn. The visit resulted in a communiqué confirming their total agreement on all major problems and indicating, for example, that they were both in favour of a fluid foreign policy; that is to say, of conversations with Mr Khruschev.

In addition to this, after an allusion to de Gaulle's Anglo-phobia, the *Daily Telegraph* wrote: 'The solitary path followed by President de Gaulle has given Britain and Germany a new responsibility for forming a closer partnership for cooperation with Washington.'

A prospect here of a 'Directory of Three'.

But more was to follow.

On December 1st in Washington, where he attended the state funeral of President Kennedy, the Chancellor declared on one of the American television circuits: 'Germany is convinced that *her existence, her security and her future*[1] are based on the alliance with the United States.'

On his return to Bonn he confirmed, on December 3rd, his '*unconditional confidence* in the alliance with the United States', the need for *a political union of Europe,* for *maintaining the closest ties with the countries of the free world* and of *making the Atlantic Alliance as strong as possible.* He also asserted his *unconditional confidence in the protection of the United States.* Finally, in reply to a question, he declined the honour of mediating between France and the United States.

On December 5th, his Foreign Minister, Herr Shroeder, declared

[1] These italics, and those that follow, are mine.

before the assembly of WEU[1] that cooperation [the ultimate goal for de Gaulle] *is not a goal in itself but a preliminary step towards the political unity of Europe.* He recalled that the Franco-German Treaty spoke of a single objective, *United Europe,* and he added: '*We must never forget this.*' He repeated: 'European political union is essential.' Paying homage to the late President Kennedy, who proposed a multilateral nuclear force, he demanded a *closely integrated* NATO defence.

These contradictions of agreements which de Gaulle had repeated on a dozen occasions occurred in the very year of the signing of the Franco-German Treaty. It is true to say that they voiced the opinions of an almost unanimous German Parliament.

Erhard at the Johnson Ranch.

Erhard's visit to the American President on his Texas ranch was a decisive step forward for Germany in international affairs. The two men found that they were in complete harmony on the major issues. In Johnson's view Erhard is the man who has made the most powerful military contribution to NATO in a spirit of complete cooperation. He is the man with whom America can come to an understanding.[2] Kennedy's great plan of economic association with Europe is consonant with the ideas which Erhard has always defended. He has never wanted Europe to remain cowering timorously in a corner.

The German-American honeymoon took place under the Texan sky, an unprecedented event in the diplomatic history of the United States! The German Chancellor was made to put on a huge Texan hat and to sing a German version of *Deep in the Heart of Texas.*

The communiqué released to the press on December 29th, 1963, dealt with all the important issues, including the following points, on which the Chancellor and the American President are in agreement, as distinct from the views of de Gaulle:

To explore every possibility of improving East-West relations.

To increase the strength and efficiency of the Atlantic alliance.

To unite Europe in order to bring this about.

To expand international trade, particularly in agricultural produce, by starting immediate negotiations in this respect.

To promote close cooperation of all members within the framework

[1] Western European Union, of which Great Britain is a member.
[2] Particularly as he reflects popular feeling, according to a recent gallup poll in January, 1964, which revealed that the Germans considered him to be a satisfactory chancellor, only 1 per cent being against him (10 per cent had no opinion).

E

of NATO so that the organisation can be prepared to meet any emergency.

Even de Gaulle could hardly take exception to the following clauses:

An American pledge to maintain six divisions in Germany.

A German promise to offset expenditure in marks of US armed forces in Germany by the purchase of American war material.

The conclusion to be drawn is the growing stake of the United States and of Germany in an ever closer association of *all the free countries* in Europe and throughout the world.

Johnson and Erhard, particularly the latter, made considerable progress in the heart of Texas, for although the following piece of news did not appear in the communiqué—possibly, it has been claimed, so that a denial could be issued in the event of an excessively violent reaction in Paris—it was published by the world press who received it from the spokesmen of the two delegations. It was confirmed by the Chancellor in the course of a press conference: 'The setting up of a committee of German and American representatives who will undertake, on a short-term basis, *a thorough examination of the clauses of the agreements signed in Brussels on December* 23rd 1963'.[1] Herr Erhard made it clear that 'this organisation would not try to seek new methods, but rather to interpret the meaning of these agreements and to define, naturally within this context, to what extent they took into account American expectations'. He added that the agreements were not 'rigid' and that *they left the door open for negotiations.* The conclusion must be that the explanations given by the head of the Federal Government had not yet completely allayed the fears entertained by American agricultural experts after the December 23rd meeting. The procedure adopted was quite unusual, being contrary to the spirit of the European Economic Community, which in principle objects to any discussions affecting it between one of its members and a third country. In Paris, where great importance is attached to the idea of a common stand on the parts of the EEC countries towards the 'Kennedy round' of tariff discussions, the setting up of the Committee evidently had a bad reception.

André Fontaine, reporting this, added:[2]

'It appears after all that the two conversationalists of the "L. B. Johnson ranch" decided to give a new impulse to German-American collaboration which, during the latter part of Dr Adenauer's term in office, had cooled off somewhat. They agreed to keep in touch chiefly by

[1] When the Common Market determined the agricultural tariff policy of Europe.
[2] *Le Monde*, December 31st, 1963.

correspondence, and the Chancellor referred openly to the possibility of more frequent personal meetings. Hardly had he returned home than he made a point of announcing that new efforts were needed to reconcile divergent views in Western Europe to bring about its unification so that it could become a true partner of the United States. "Our good relations with France," he said a few hours earlier as he boarded his plane, "do not in any way compete with our friendship for the United States, which is such a vital factor for us. President Johnson," he added, "had also stressed how much he hoped we should maintain harmonious relations with France." This confirms the impression that far from forcing Germany to make a choice between Paris and Washington, the White House is counting far more on the influence of the Federal Republic in persuading its French ally to show a more conciliatory attitude.'

The extraordinary success of this meeting was stressed by the Washington correspondent of London's *Sunday Times* under the headline: 'Germany now joins special relations'. This would take the form of a Directory of Three with the United States and Great Britain. De Gaulle had asked Eisenhower in 1958 to create such a Directory with France and Great Britain, the latter already enjoying preferential treatment. Eisenhower had refused.

There was no doubt, according to this article, that since this sensational meeting the identity of views between Washington and Bonn was greater than between Washington and London. And it wondered whether some anxiety was not felt in London as to the effects which this new fact might have on the longstanding and special Anglo-American relationships. Presumably none was felt because the leading article in the same issue bore the headlines: 'The Triple Alliance'. The alliance, of course, comprised Germany, Great Britain and the United States.

The article praised Professor Erhard as a good, moderate, reasonable and sympathetic statesman. 'With France temporarily so intransigent, it is inevitable that any American government which wants to do business in Europe should do business with Germany.'

The author of this leader maintained that this triple alliance could work even if the Labour Party won the election, for Harold Wilson regards himself as an 'Atlantic' rather than a 'European' politician.

Mr Dean Acheson would have been justified in smiling to see his advice followed. But it is hardly a laughing matter for France.

It remained for the Chancellor to reply to the proud declaration ('I reject American protection') that had been made by de Gaulle the previous September. In his budget speech to the Bundestag in January, 1964,

131

the Chancellor spoke with sound common sense on the subject of his country's relations with the United States: 'We are not an American protectorate, but I am ready to accept this description in the sense that our security depends upon the United States.'

One can understand the comment published in *Die Welt* on January 2nd: 'We are faced with the difficult task of preventing our alliance with the greatest power in the world from harming our friendship for France.'

But they give priority to the greatest power in the world.

15th January, 1964. *Erhard in London, Segni in Washington.*

One day after the anniversary of de Gaulle's veto, Chancellor Erhard, during his visit to London, took the opposite view to de Gaulle's press conference. Erhard began by saying: 'There can be no prosperous, happy and free Europe unless Great Britain is part of it.'

Of Europe—without Great Britain—as a third force between the United States and Soviet Russia he said: 'Europe without Great Britain is a myth and not a political reality. In order for Europe to play her part in the world and make her influence felt, the whole of Europe must act as a community of free and equal nations.'

Going further than President Kennedy, who had only spoken of a partnership, he asserted (and what a contrast to de Gaulle's attitude): 'The Atlantic *community* is indispensable if we wish to survive in a world of strife and tension. If we pool our resources and stand together we shall be the winners in the future.'

The communiqué insisted that NATO must remain a pivot of the Western offensive organisation and confirmed the agreement between London and Bonn to carry through the Kennedy negotiations on the lowering of world tariffs.

In Washington on the same day, January 1st, Signor Segni, President of the Italian Republic, defended the same political ideas before Congress. He said: 'We must, as soon as possible, create the *Atlantic partnership*, and to this end bring about, within the framework of NATO, *a united Europe*. If Europe wishes to become strong she must be *united politically*, for a divided Europe would soon appear out-of-date and anachronistic.'

Yes, but there is de Gaulle . . .

The Italian Foreign Minister, Signor Saragat, insisted: 'A Europe without Great Britain is inconceivable.' In Washington he said: 'Italy is in favour of a united Europe. Any attempt at a hegemony will fail *just as the so-called Paris-Bonn axis has already failed*. It would be the same with any plan tending to alienate Europe from the United States.' He ended with these words: 'We shall make the greatest effort to overcome or suppress the difficulties created by France.'

The final communiqué on the exchange of views between Chancellor Erhard and the British Prime Minister, published on January 16th, 1964, announced agreement between the two governments on the three following points:

(1) The Western alliance *must continue its efforts to try to lessen the tension between East and West.*

(2) NATO must remain the keystone of Western defence.

(3) A reaffirmation of the unity of Europe '*on a foundation which has been broadly established*'.

Thus, among all the European leaders, there is only one who is out of step with the rest. The Chancellor is in agreement with all the others. Alas, Arnold Toynbee was right!

CHAPTER 19

De Gaulle reverses France's foreign policy

'*France's foreign policy has undergone a revolution.*'

U THANT.

Secretary General to the United Nations.

WHAT KIND OF REVOLUTION IS THIS? SIMPLY THE REVERSAL OF France's traditional policy of union with Great Britain and the United States, who have the same ideals as ourselves—democracy and the defence of national freedom.

Since the inevitable refusal to accept a Directory of Three, the no-less inevitable rejection of his proposal for a three-power supervised peace in the Belgian Congo and his disappointment over the Moscow Treaty, we have seen de Gaulle break away from NATO, deliver public attacks on the United States, and issue a call to the under-developed nations (this too was a shot at America). His first action in this respect was, as we have seen, to suggest that the Americans should leave South Vietnam. Now came the second.

China recognised.

De Gaulle forgets that only recently he depicted the 'Yellow Peril' in lurid terms: 'Vast, poverty-stricken China . . . casting an eye on territories which one day she will find it necessary to overrun.' Yet now, with an unerring sense of drama, he decided to recognise Communist China. This was a direct blow against America, which had lost 54,000 men killed in Korea, with 103,000 wounded, and to date has lost 210 men killed in South Vietnam, in an effort to prevent China extending her domination, either by propaganda or force of arms. For the United States, Communist China is the enemy, and now de Gaulle has recognised China. What a sorry picture of disagreement between allies. The

West, dealt this body blow, is dismayed; the Communists in the Chinese camp are triumphant, and the underdeveloped countries are amused and gratified.

No objection can be raised to the principle of recognising a government which has effectively governed Continental China for fifteen years. Lunching three years ago with my friend Mr Kenneth Galbraith, author of *The Affluent Society*, then President Kennedy's economic adviser and later American ambassador in India, I asked him: 'Don't you think it would be better if China entered the United Nations before she possesses the atomic bomb rather than after?' He replied that he entirely agreed with me.

This means that I am not opposed in principle to the recognition of China. But since then an event of major importance has occurred. Attacked and insulted by China, Russia has drawn nearer to the West, signing the Moscow Treaty with all the nations of the world apart from China, Albania and France. Was this an auspicious moment to recognise China, which condemns Russia for having chosen the path of peaceful co-existence with us, in other words for refusing to destroy us in a genocidal war? Moreover America, our great ally in Europe, is also our ally in South-east Asia, where she has taken over France's responsibilities in the interests of democracy and freedom in South Vietnam. France is also a member of SEATO, whose members have undertaken 'to declare publicly and formally their sense of unity', and are pledged 'to coordinate their efforts for collective defence' and 'to achieve the objectives of the treaty . . . by means of continuous self-help and mutual aid'.

Questioned by the press on January 27th, 1964, about the recognition of China, I quoted the SEATO Treaty and asked: 'Does our vaunted independence mean neglecting our engagements to our allies?' For we have recognised China without having negotiated with our allies. And are we likely to stop there? Since China exists should she not be admitted to UNO, to be a member of the Security Council, and to have the right of veto?

World opinion.

United States: The White House and State Department policy is to conceal the true feelings which the French action has aroused. These are easy to guess. 'Even Congress will not reveal the full extent of its anger,' wrote Alain Clément in *Le Monde*.

Congressional opinion is of importance to the French leader,

135

Raymond Cartier tells us in *Paris-Match*;[1] since American public opinion is so powerful, he continues, the members of Congress, through their
public contacts, accurately reflect popular opinion. What is being said
in Congress? The general feeling can be summed up in a single phrase:
'De Gaulle has stabbed America in the back'. America is fighting
South-east Asia to check the spread of Communist influence throughout
Asia—and France hurries to the aid of Chinese Communism. The words
'provocation' and 'treachery' have been heard in the precincts of
the Capitol.

'Those who inspire or direct American diplomacy,' adds Rayond
Cartier, 'do not need much pressing to speak their minds: *"General de
Gaulle has committed France to a dead-end policy*.[2] He has neither the military
nor the financial means, nor the necessary alliances to sustain it."

'*The preliminary condition* for a discussion on an equal footing with
America, was *a political and economically united Europe*. Washington experts
consider that the chances of such a union are dead and will never be
revived . . . Today America's real policy is to maintain and foster the
Balkanisation of Europe . . . Having failed to maintain her impetus
towards union, Europe has lapsed into her old divisions. Faced with this
dismembered Europe, America has no further worry . . . It goes without
saying that the capital where the recognition of China has aroused
greatest resentment is Moscow . . . French policy has created a new bond
between Moscow and Washington.'

No comment is needed. But there are many of us in Europe who refuse
to accept what might be called 'Europe deceased'.

The Republicans agree with the Democrats regarding the French
action. Eisenhower has said that France's recognition of Peking is 'a
monumental error', while former Vice-President Nixon stated on
January 20th, 1964, in Philadelphia, that the United States must give
'a new slant' to their foreign policy particularly regarding *Latin America
and France, who represents 'a new vision of Europe'*.

New York Times, January 17th, 1964. C. L. Sulzberger wrote: 'We
had been so careful to explain how disconcerting to American interests
it would be were France to acknowledge Mao Tse-tung's regime now
that it is clear de Gaulle knew he risked jeopardising his trans-Atlantic
relationships by this deliberate step. Presumably he didn't care.'
Sulzberger pointed out that there was no comparison with Great
Britain's action immediately after Mao Tse-tung's victory. Britain

[1] February 8th, 1964.
[2] These, and other italics in Cartier's article are mine.

exchanged embassies with Peking and left a consul in Taiwan before the bloody Korean war.

New York Daily News, January 22nd, 1964. (Republican.)

'The French Government yesterday rejected, bluntly if not rudely, the US government's protest against President Charles de Gaulle's announced intention to recognise Red China.'

New York Herald Tribune, January 23rd, 1964. (Independent Republican.)

'President de Gaulle started the new year with a bang. He developed his diplomatic offensive in Asia by offering arms to Cambodia and by negotiating diplomatic recognition of Red China. *He is now opening a "second front" in Latin America.* His attraction, of course, is his new image as the *leader of a revolt against the United States* . . . The trouble with de Gaulle's neutralism is that it may do nothing to save countries which already are neutral (countries such as Cambodia and Laos are in no need of conversion by de Gaulle), but that it may do a good deal to weaken independent countries and ripen them for Communism.'

New York Times, January 28th, 1964. (Independent.)

'Ever since 1958 the French President has been seeking American acceptance of a world-power role for France and formulation of a joint American-British-French global strategy. Our refusal to discuss this seriously with him has led to a series of Gaullist moves against American policy in NATO, the Common Market, Soviet-Western negotiations and, now, Asia.'

New York Herald Tribune, January 28th, 1964.

'De Gaulle hopes for a neutralised South-east Asia in which France will hold the balance between the two great contestants; the United States and Communist China. It is in this context that French recognition of Peking must be viewed. Unfortunately, the idea of a third force, operating for peace in South-east Asia, is one that has been tried before with poor results . . . *But France's "two Chinas" solution may have some more immediate, practical and tragic effects.* The lure of neutralism in South-east Asia, riven as it is by Chinese-sponsored civil war, may weaken the opposition to Communism. Nor is it only in Asia that the French have given a lift to the wrong side. In Africa, in South America, wherever a potential or actual revolutionary situation exists, the most violent draw inspiration and help from Red China. *France's countenance to this source of rebellion may yet plague France itself.*'

New York Daily News, January 28th, 1964.

'General de Gaulle . . . is as unpredictable as he is brave and patriotic.

137

We only hope he hasn't started Red China on the road toward enormous power in the world—which may one day drag the United States into a war to save the Soviet Union, Western Europe, *and most definitely France*, from being overrun by Chinese Red hordes. *We have saved France twice from the Germans. Let's hope we don't eventually have to save it from the Chinese.*'
New York Herald Tribune, January 30th, 1964.

'De Gaulle hopes that the Communists in Asia will call a halt to their "wars of liberation". But for the Communists *neutralisation can only represent a pause before the total control by Communism. As old admirers of General de Gaulle we are distressed to see him pursue this plan.* We cannot see how it can help France since the fact of dealing with Communism has never helped anyone or any decent nation. This can do a great deal of harm to Franco-American relations.'
New York Herald Tribune, February 1st, 1964.

'If South-east Asia is to be neutralised, Red China is not the only entity to be consulted. Indeed it is rather surprising that de Gaulle did not begin his campaign by *consulting his allies rather than by approaching an enemy.* We suggest that the French President has started at the wrong end. Before recognising Peking, he might have recognised Washington and London.'

And here are a few enthusiastic articles. The *Washington Post* (Independent), on February 1st wrote: 'President de Gaulle's record as a prophet is better than most. As he has done before, the tall Frenchman may be leading our eyes to shores still dimly seen. Though this country may differ with France, it would be folly to refuse to take seriously the sonorous words of the greatest of Frenchmen.'

The French radio and press seized eagerly upon the article in *Newsweek* of February 10th. It is relevant to mention that on December 30th the same weekly published, beneath a cartoon representing a back view of de Gaulle with elbows spread, one finger stuck in each ear, a leading article entitled: '*A man of firm opinions*'. It began as follows: 'The mystification felt by Charles de Gaulle's allies when they try to fathom his intentions towards NATO or the Common Market is a sensation intimately familiar to Frenchmen.'

The article of February 10th, illustrated by a cartoon showing an Asia with de Gaulle's profile was entitled: '*France: A Return to Greatness*'. The sub-title is as follows: '*Satisfied with conditions at home, Charles de Gaulle now projects himself onto the world scene as Europe's self-appointed spokesman*'.

Speaking of de Gaulle's influence the author quotes this admission from a high Italian official: 'I'm afraid we Europeans are going through a dishonest phase . . . Gaullism is now a trans-European philosophy.' A Dutch aviation executive said to him: 'The US should understand we are not being anti-American in hoping de Gaulle succeeds . . . But Europe must now organise itself and think of the future, of opening up new markets—which, of course, implies new relations.' This is hardly an appeal to the uncommitted nations! He proceeded to maintain that one of de Gaulle's cardinal principles is to create difficulties for Washington, wherever possible . . . The United States has reacted to all this with a mixture of suppressed fury and calculated indifference, convinced that Gaullism will die with de Gaulle . . .' He also insisted that de Gaulle is the greatest disciple of Machiavelli; this is justified by what he managed to do to the Constitution after having it approved by the French.

The author of the article then speaks in flattering terms of the French recovery, which official propaganda has publicised so widely that it is unnecessary to repeat it here.

The same day, *Time*, another American magazine, justly praised the personal qualities of Couve de Murville and also spoke warmly of the French recovery.

Great Britain: Official government reaction was as follows. We fear that by appearing to want to rival the United States in the Far East, France, who has neither the military nor the financial means, may weaken the global position of the West.

Daily Telegraph, February 1st, 1964.

'President de Gaulle's voice is calm, his language dignified, even noble. Yet practically every word he utters might have been carefully calculated to offend susceptibility, or prick some illusion, or blast some hope, or confound some policy dear to one or other or all his allies. He made it quite clear yesterday that he still believes in a European union which is small, which is not in any real or supranational sense united, which is uncommitted to America. This Europe, making as it does the worst of at least three possible worlds, happens to be desired by none of his friends, whether in or out of the Six. No matter: he desires it. It is enough . . . He has recognised Communist China, as we indeed have long done. We have not profited by doing so; will he?'

The Guardian, February 3rd, 1964.

'The most obvious motives . . . would be those behind his announced policy for a neutral South-east Asia—*a challenge to American supremacy mixed with a desire to give the world the benefits of France's greatness and wisdom*. The Americans, however they might view his new Asia policy, will be only too glad to share with him some of the burdens of the Alliance for Progress.[1] But with a gross national product only one eighth that of the United States, the impact in real terms of France's additional assistance cannot be very marked . . .'

Germany: West Germany intends to remain a faithful ally of the United States. The Federal Government announced this in restrained but firm tones in its communiqué of January 27th. It recalled as a start that it had often stressed *the need for maintaining Western unity* and added: 'This is why we should have preferred France's decision and its consequences to be *discussed within the framework of the Western Community.* The Federal Government hopes that the step taken by France will cause *no damage to the free world and* the cohesion of the Western Powers.' What a lesson!

Die Welt of Hamburg, February 1st, 1946. (Independent.)

'This time Charles de Gaulle has appeared on the scene as a *dictatorial international arbitrator* who appraises world affairs and puts them in their true perspective. The tone in which he shows continental Europe what he considers to be the realistic and attractive way forward is haughty, almost condescending. As usual de Gaulle has put forward no concrete proposals. His invitation now for political collaboration in Europe leaves the door open to all possibilities. It is, however, clear cut: *Great Britain and the United States are obviously faced with a new "no".'*

Neue Ruhr Zeitung of Essen. February 1st, 1964. (Social Democrat.)

'Whatever the outcome, de Gaulle, with his risky poker game in South-east Asia, has struck such a blow at American policy that it is permissible to wonder once more if this France, led by de Gaulle, can still be considered an ally of Washington.'

Kolnische Rundschau, January 28th, 1964. (Christian Democrat.)

'For Germany the alliance with the United States is an important and necessary as friendship with France. We have to tread the narrow path of cooperation between the two States. *This becomes more and more difficult* every day.'

Austria: Der Express of Vienna, January 27th, 1964.

'The French initiative entails a dangerous illusion for the Chinese, *i.e. that the Western camp is divided and that it is still possible for a Communist country to play-off one of the countries of the free world against another.'*

Italy: Il Popolo. January 23rd, 1964. (Christian Democrat.)

'By recognising Red China, de Gaulle, at the cost of further upsetting relations with NATO, Bonn and Washington, pretending to be the leading spirit in a world game, is really endangering a genuine solution

[1] An Association of American States financed by the United States.

of the basic problem of China as a factor in international affairs and is once more complicating the question of her recognition.'

Switzerland: The Geneva Tribune, January 29th, 1964.

Referring to the recognition of Communist China by the French Government, the paper stated that 'the latter is proud of an initiative which allows her to play a large-scale role in Asiatic politics. But this initiative will only be of advantage to the Communist powers. *If there be any greatness it is only in the magnitude of the gift she has made them.*'

The Geneva Tribune, January 31st, 1964.

'Mr Khruschev is pleased with France's recognition of Peking . . . Paris in fact is carrying out a policy constantly preached by the Kremlin and *is sowing discord in the Atlantic camp*. Moscow could not ask for anything better.' (J. J. Chouet.)

Poland: Zycie Warsawy, January 21st, 1964.

'To begin with it is not only today that General de Gaulle distinguishes himself by his political realism, which encourages him to abandon the old, futile, diplomatic formulae. It is well to remember, for example, that de Gaulle was the first, and so far the only, Western statesman to declare himself as early as 1959 *in favour of the recognition of the Oder-Niesse line . . . Finally, de Gaulle seizes every opportunity to display his independence with regard to the policies of Washington.*'

Hungary: Hetfoi Hirek of Budapest. January 27th, 1964.

'The Élysée's plans to recover the ascendancy in Asia are the key to France's recognition of China. Furthermore, French capital is looking for new outlets.'

Africa: Al Akhbar of Cairo. February 1st, 1964.

'*The French head of State has defied the United States* and ridiculed her in his exposition . . . The recent coup in South Vietnam was prepared when they felt the growing influence of the General's partisans in Saigon. The General has also defied the United States and her policies in Europe, Africa and Latin America.'

Hong Kong: Hong Kong Standard. January 29th, 1964.

'De Gaulle has quite clearly reaffirmed his independence in foreign policy, but what profit will he draw from it in the last analysis? For Peking the operation appears far more dividend-paying. China's recognition by Paris, from this point of view, is the greatest change that has taken place for the past ten years. It represents not only *a considerable victory for Mao Tse-tung*, but also an event which *opens the way to other diplomatic successes*. The advantage which Peking will gain from the French decision will doubtless strengthen Mao Tse-tung's position in his differences with Khruschev; this may not be altogether to the taste of the Soviet leader.'

North Vietnam: Nhan Dan of Hanoi. January 30th, 1964.

'The fact that France has recognised Communist China, despite the opposition of the United States, represents a setback for that Power's policy.'

South Vietnam: A vigorous official protest.

The South Vietnamese Press agency, January 20th, 1964.

'Now France once again contemplates to make her re-entry into the Far Eastern scene by coming to terms with the Communist Peking regime at the expense of the Vietnam peoples' interests . . . As a price for the deal Peking will ask for the recognition of Communist China by France. Recognition of Peking by France in the present international contest, far from checking Communist China's penetration into Southeast Asia, as was claimed by competent French circles, on the contrary favours the enterprise of Communist China which aims at dominating this part of the world.'

The same agency on January 28th, 1964, relayed an official protest from the Saigon Government which reserved the right to take any measures it saw fit to deal with the situation: 'If France is free to decide on its attitude regarding the Chinese problem, it none the less remains that the decision which the French Government had just taken bears directly on Vietnam, which has been engaged in the merciless fight against the Communist aggression for over nine years. It is proper to recall that that fight, which had its origin in France's imperialist policy, has led by its fault to the abandonment of half the territory of Vietnam to the Communists, thus sacrificing the national interest of the Vietnamese people.'

India: The official reaction is that the recognition of China has come ten years too late or five years too early.

The *Times of India* felt that the border conflict with China prevented India from giving her wholehearted approval.

Malaysia: The *Straits Times* of Kuala Lumpur, January 28th, 1964.

'France possesses neither the deterrent of the Seventh Fleet nor the vast global power which the United States can instantly mobilise. While there may be much to criticise in American policy in South Vietnam, Laos and Cambodia, French ambitions and policies can win the sympathy only of those who believe—as Prince Sihanouk does—that Southeast Asia is lost to Communism in the long-run and that a brief respite is all that can be hoped for.'

Philippines: Manila Daily Bulletin, January 29th, 1964.

'*South Vietnam and South Korea will be the countries most affected by the French decision,* for this recognition will certainly raise the prestige of the warlike aggressor and *will raise doubts among those who are waging such a desperate fight as to the wisdom of their struggle.*'

Australia: Melbourne Age, January 29th, 1964.

'*Australia cannot contemplate turning away from America at this moment simply to follow the fashion set by France.*'

Syria: Al Jaryda of Beirut, January 28th, 1964.

'President de Gaulle has scored again in his conflict with the White House. Quite apart from the favourable reaction given by the whole world to France's decision, *which places this country once more in the forefront of international politics,* it must be admitted that France has used the Chinese dragon, which even frightens the men of Moscow.'

Chile: El Mercurio of Santiago da Chile, January 29th, 1964.

'The initiative taken by France in recognising Communist China, and the French statement that Communist China can co-exist with the West, whereas it is well known that Chinese Communist policy is frankly hostile to the Western world, are *disconcerting and distressing. The French decision has broken the Western front, weakened its unity and mutual understanding and threatened its policies.*'

Cuba: La Tarde of Havana, January 28th, 1964.

'The establishment of diplomatic relations between France and Communist China is *proof of good sense and intelligence. This decision has been greatly resented by the Yankees, although it has aroused world-wide satisfaction.*'

These were some typical reactions around the world. It is easy to see who was grieved and who rejoiced.

January 31st, 1964. Press Conference: The Constitution, Europe and the uncommitted nations.

If world interest had been aroused by the previous day's announcement of the recognition of Communist China, this conference, purely from the technical angle, was a remarkable performance: a 90-minute harangue by the Head of State to 1,000 French and foreign journalists, without a single glance at his notes. He spoke passionately on two subjects—the Constitution and Europe. On both issues he defended his actions.

In times past the Constitution, like scripture, commanded respect. For de Gaulle it is merely a 'spirit'. Thus, contrary to its clearest mandate, he has claimed the right to supreme powers. The regime he describes is closer to that of the Sun King than to that of the document accepted by 80% of Frenchmen—despite the fact that the principle of the separation of powers already existed then, and that this impediment seems today to have been removed. In the study I shall be publishing on this subject it will be seen that Prime Minister Pompidou and I are in agreement in saying that the referendum of October, 1962, which decreed that the Head of State would in future be elected by universal suffrage, *did not, on the contrary, increase his very modest powers.* It is worth noting that a law student who, in front of an examiner, described the powers of a Head of State as de Gaulle did to 1,000 journalists, would undoubtedly be failed.

On the subject of a politically integrated Europe, de Gaulle, annoyed at having nobody to share his views, takes great pains to try to split his opponents in the Common Market, whom he reproaches for wanting either 'deliberately to put Europe back *under America's thumb*' or 'to confine it to the realm of brilliant subjects for political declarations, without ever bringing it into being'.

He is only right in saying that the demand for integration under supranational control, to which he is opposed, *but without which there would be no Europe*, is incompatible with the presence of Great Britain, who is in fact welcomed by his opponents, since this is what we must now call our five Common Market partners. This, then, is the confusion which has arisen due to the obstinate way in which he has blocked the way to European unity.

When he accuses his opponents of trying to place Europe under America's thumb, he is making an odd mistake, for when President Johnson received Chancellor Erhard he had bitter things to say about the Ministers of the six European countries, who on the previous December 23rd had in principle decided to persuade Europe to buy French wheat at a high price rather than the cheaper American commodity. The 'chicken war' has shown Europe's capacity for defending herself. What then would happen were Europe to be really united, with someone to speak in her name?

This aggressive attitude towards America was the outstanding feature of his press conference. De Gaulle has made his choice: he has raised the standard of revolt on behalf of the poor and downtrodden against rich and powerful America—like a rich member of the middle classes joining an extreme left wing party. The revolutionaries cheer him, delighted that he has been seduced. It is only too true that France's foreign policy has been reversed.

And here two questions spring to mind. Is it possible to live under the American umbrella and to campaign against your benefactor? Is this in keeping with French tradition?

On January 31st, at his press conference, de Gaulle's appeal to the under-developed countries was shrouded, almost swamped in generalities, but an article by Jean Daniel[1], which earned the approval of the UNR, UDT paper, *Notre République*, threw some light on his ideas.

This is how Jean Daniel described the *great plan*: 'Spurned in the United States and challenged in Europe[2], General de Gaulle has achieved his objectives—to see to it that in the free world France is to be reckoned with, and that she is considered by the East as a spokesman to be treated with respect.'

It is highly doubtful whether the great powers of the 'free world', indignant at this change of face, or Mr Khruschev, exasperated for more than a year by the Franco-German Treaty, will reckon any more with the France of today than with the France of yesterday.

One thing is certain: in the under-developed countries the spectacle of David defying the American Goliath has aroused some enthusiasm for de Gaulle. Jean Daniel considers *that the sole reason for de Gaulle's success* with these nations is his attitude towards America. In the eyes of the under-developed nations, he said, 'this is *a real revolution* . . . History may undervalue the Constitution, ignore the collapse of the French army and even pronounce varied judgments on the restoration of peace in Algeria. *It will remember this gigantic challenge to an alliance* . . .'

This may prove true but history will doubtless also add: 'To abandon powerful allies, the only allies capable of balancing Soviet power, merely to gain the applause of the under-developed nations, however comforting this may be, is a fool's game. The hallmark of a statesman, as opposed to dictators, is not to court popularity.'

On the other hand I agree with Jean Daniel when he wrote: 'one can say with Professor Vedel that Gaullist reaction is an immature reaction. This is very true.'

If this is true, as I fear it is, I feel humiliated for my country for we do not suffer from poverty, which is the sole excuse for jealousy.

This 'revolution' is a crime to the extent that it weakens the defence of the free world; it also shows ingratitude towards our allies of two wars.

Jean Daniel concludes that de Gaulle considers involvement in any scheme whatsoever *with the United States* means *to become engulfed*. NATO

---

[1] '*Le Mythe Gaulliste dans le Tiers Monde*', *Le Monde*, February 5th, 1964.
[2] The word 'challenged' is weak since we have seen de Gaulle in disagreement with all our partners on essentials.

is one of these systems. Does he intend to leave it? One can see where this political thinking would lead France. To be afraid of 'becoming engulfed' indicates an inferiority complex which certainly does not exist today in Germany; it is very surprising to find it in a man who is the very epitome of courage. In twenty years' time, when there are a thousand million Chinese, our descendants will be amazed to realize that in 1964 there was a statesman who, as deliberate policy, could consider dividing the white races.

CHAPTER 20   *Why so many mistakes?*

WHY HAVE THERE BEEN SO MANY MISTAKES?

Why impede the progress towards the United Europe which Robert Schuman and then the Treaty of Rome got under way?

Why this refusal to participate loyally in the defence of Europe, within the framework of NATO?

Why scoff at the United Nations?

Why this obstinate refusal to speak to Mr Khruschev, talking all the while about 'Europe from the Atlantic to the Urals'?

Why this affront to Great Britain, whose courage in the war saved us, after we had signed an armistice which lost our entire fleet to the allied cause?

Why this mistrust, this hostility, this malice towards the United States to whom we owe our very freedom?

What is the meaning of a solemn treaty with Germany, if our policy is directly opposed to hers on all major issues?

Why was the Constitution first twisted and later violated, the Council of State threatened and a tribunal dissolved because the judges proved intractable?

De Gaulle constantly repeats that France needs continuity. Alas, France has continuity today but of what a kind!

There are reasons for so many grave mistakes.

The first and deepest, of course, is General de Gaulle's brand of patriotism: 'France in the front rank'—an illusion which breeds further illusions.

But of course there are other reasons as well. One can be a great

147

man without being a statesman. A real statesman must be familiar with the facts about the world in which he lives. We have seen that de Gaulle is uninformed on many essentials. But is this his fault? He forged a brilliant career for himself in the army. Could he possibly have supplemented it with the training provided by a long parliamentary career? Compare the development of de Gaulle with that of Churchill, who entered the House of Commons at the beginning of the century, who learned about public affairs as President of the Board of Trade, Home Secretary, Chancellor of the Exchequer and First Lord of the Admiralty—to mention only a few of his early government posts. To have taken part for so many years in so many debates, on so many different subjects, to have been subjected to a host of diametrically opposed views both in the House and in the lobbies—is not all this more valuable equipment for a politician than a keen military mind?

This is the reason for de Gaulle's failure to appreciate the realities of world politics today.

Politics is a difficult art.

But, it might be argued, he could be informed by his colleagues. Very true, but is he prepared to accept their advice? When I think of him I always recall the words of Fenelon concerning Louis XIV: 'The gap around the throne terrifies me.'

When de Gaulle produced his draft Constitution depriving the members of Parliament of their powers and replacing them by officials who were presumably considered to be more amenable, I asked him: 'Do you think that the head of a ministry would have led the British people so well during the war as Winston Churchill?' He merely replied: 'There are very few Churchills.' Probably he was already thinking that supreme power should be the prerogative of the President—namely himself.

The Constitutional Consultative Committee suggested that instead of suspending the members of Parliament belonging to the government, he should discharge them during the time they were members of it. The point of this was to prevent them voting for the government of which they were members.

De Gaulle refused, and by the way in which he applied the Constitution, provided us with our present hybrid regime.

But, you will say, we have the Council of Ministers.

The present government is largely comprised of high-ranking civil servants. Ministers who, anxious about their future, were elected deputies for the first time in 1962, and who resigned the following day in order to remain ministers, can hardly be called parliamentarians. Would any ministers with parliamentary experience, in touch with the people and familiar with the course of events, make the mistake of ordering 300,000 miners back to work, only to give way later?[1] Would they have allowed him to get mixed up in the 'lobster war', supported by a warship which had to beat an inglorious retreat?

The qualities of his ministers are well-known; but their idea of administration seems to be confined merely to giving their views on measures likely to be in the public interest, then leaving it to the government alone to make decisions, with which they are bound to agree.

A politician who has taken a stand on important issues will not meekly stand by and see them repudiated by the government of which he is a member. Antoine Pinay resigned over foreign policy, as did Pierre Pflimlin and his colleagues of the MRP over Europe. They acted in true parliamentary tradition.

But, it may be argued, there is still Parliament. True, but it hardly counts any more, because, by insinuating himself between Parliament and the people, by making full use of his oratorical and dramatic gifts on television (which he monopolises), de Gaulle has a direct hold on the people from whom the members of Parliament derive their power.

If de Gaulle continues to make mistakes it is because no one has the power to enlighten him by contradicting him. His greatest enemy is his prestige—abroad as well as in France.

When he spoke at Westminster both Lords and Commons were enthusiastic; in New York, driving along Broadway, he was given the ticker-tape treatment; in Germany he had such an ovation that the security services wondered anxiously if he was not going to revive the personality cult. His triumphs abroad deceive him and give him a false idea of his power. In France they encourage him to plunge more deeply into error. And after the errors come the bitter repudiations. One thinks of Saint-Beuve's judgment on Guizot[2]: 'What destroyed him were his oratorical triumphs'.

Alas, de Gaulle's personal tragedy is also the tragedy of France. For France is the victim of all these mistakes.

---

[1] Early in 1963 the mine-workers came out on strike. De Gaulle peremptorily ordered them to return to work. They refused and the government had to back down.

[2] François Guizot (1787–1874), statesman and historian. Premier of France 1847–1848.

CHAPTER 21   *Be a great nation once more!*

GAULLIST FOREIGN POLICY IS NOT BASED ON ANY PRINCIPLES: IT merely consists of a series of contradictory policies originally motivated by illusions and later by grudges.

First there was the illusion that France could be 'in the forefront', on a par with the American and Russian giants; and that a dismembered Europe could defend herself unaided against Soviet Russia.

An even more ridiculous illusion was the idea that such a Europe could act as arbitrator between the American and Soviet colossi.

Then there was the stubborn illusion of a Europe stretching from the Atlantic to the Urals, America being excluded.

As for the grudges, the first was against the 'Anglo-Saxons', born of bitter wartime memories and the fact that France could not be 'in the forefront' while there is America to be reckoned with.

There was also a deep-seated grudge which caused de Gaulle to say in 1950: 'Let America look after the Pacific and Great Britain the Far East,' and this at a time when America was organising the defence of a threatened Western Europe.

On his return to power in 1958 and after Eisenhower's rejection of a Directory of Three, de Gaulle became even more bitter. Now as a dissatisfied partner in the alliance he announced that France must defend herself, by herself and in her own fashion. He withdrew his fleets from NATO at the end of the Algerian war, and refused his allies an effective military contribution. Instead he went ahead with his own nuclear force, which could add nothing to the common defence effort, and would, in fact, be fraught with deadly danger for France.

Sensing his political impotence, de Gaulle, in 1963, launched his veto against Great Britain and proceeded to attack America, declaring that he would not accept their protection—without saying whom he proposed should take their place—and incited the under-developed countries to resist American influence.

We have seen what the moral implication of such a policy would be, France sheltering beneath the American 'nuclear umbrella' and at the same time raising the standard of revolt against her.

Of course we must help the uncommitted nations, but for their own sakes, and not at someone else's expense and with a view to winning popularity.

In the course of his projected tour of Latin America, de Gaulle will be wildly acclaimed, partly for his own sake but far more for his anti-Americanism. If he went to Cuba to see Fidel Castro, he would get a hysterical welcome. But once the applause died down these nations would ask themselves: can he replace the Americans? Then we would have to face the harsh reality, and the quixotic character of his mission would be uncovered.

These are the latest developments in his political wanderings.

The great European powers, our kinsmen in culture and economic development, who know that they owe their independence to American protection, will of course turn their backs on us. Are they not more valuable to us than distant applause? Only then shall we be able to assess what we have lost through this policy.

What will France's position be—this ally who forgets services rendered and refuses full and loyal cooperation in the face of the common danger? And what will be history's judgment on this bid to divide the white races, living today under the threat of a thousand million Chinese— who under the iron hand of Communism will in twenty years be one of the three Great Powers?

Alas, this is not all. Spurred by his sensitive nationalism de Gaulle has put a stop to Europe which, under French leadership, was progressing towards unity. He has also opposed his partners of the Common Market on every issue, which has allowed Germany to usurp the place which was rightly ours.

Failing to appreciate the world-wide trend towards close association, he is as hostile to the United Nations as to a United Europe, trying to prevent the nations from looking beyond their national frontiers.

This policy must be changed so that France may once more assume her rightful place in Europe and the world. De Gaulle must be prevented from toppling his own monument.

De Gaulle today is the only obstacle in the path of a unified Europe. To those who say 'this obstacle must be by-passed', history will give its assent.

A man of destiny.

I say that there must be a change of policy.

If only de Gaulle were willing and would agree to respect his own Constitution. But can he do it?

Alas, he is convinced that he cannot be wrong because it was France who summoned him. Read in his *Memoirs*[1] the account he gives of his own state of mind and that of the French people after his retirement on January 20th, 1946:

After his resignation 'that rarified atmosphere, that hope of success, that ambition for France which kept the national spirit high, all disappeared. Everyone, whatever his political views, felt deep-down that the General was taking with him something primordial, something permanent and vital, which he embodied in history and which could not be represented in the party system. *The leader who remained aloof* was seen as a kind of appointed *custodian of supreme authority*, a last resort selected in advance. It was understood that this legitimacy could remain latent during an untroubled period . . . My attitude over the course of the years was to be dictated by this mission which France continued to assign to me.'

Sixteen years later, on September 20th, 1962, de Gaulle said to the French nation on television: 'Since the French people have called upon me officially to resume my place at its head . . .'

Officially! Like Louis XVIII returning from Ghent to Paris.

Whether at Colombey or at the Élysée, de Gaulle sees himself as the legitimate leader of France. National representation comes a long way behind! He confirmed this by recalling at President Coty's funeral how the latter had summoned him:

'He counselled the tottering government to turn, like himself, to that *underlying legality*, which resides not in the *diverse, doubtful and nervous representatives of trends which divide the nation*, but rather in the hopes and institutions which, on the contrary, tend to unite it.'

Here is that 'latent legitimacy' breaking surface and hurling its

[1] *Salvation.*

contempt in the face of diverse, doubtful and nervous national representatives.

Could there be any stranger idea in modern times? But a man of destiny makes no mistakes.

De Gaulle will therefore persevere.

And what will be the result?

In politics it is essential not to lose one's honour. This means that when the nation makes a mistake it has to be told, whatever the cost of such frankness. Today it needs courage to say to the French people: the famous man who governs you is mistaken. What is more, he is wrong on all major issues.

A dangerous undertaking?

But, you may say, this would be an almost hopeless struggle and not without danger. Remember that with his unmatched talent on television, of which he has the monopoly, de Gaulle has entry into every home and all the means of official propaganda at his command.

I was often reminded of this when I decided to write this book. To which I replied: 'That's possible, but was it not dangerous before the war to recommend a ruthless devaluation of the franc, which the highest state officials and the entire press cried down and which earned me death threats from angry bank depositors?

'Was it not dangerous in 1924 to challenge our so-called military glory, successive war ministers and the entire Parliament by calling for an offensive army, and later, during the five years prior to the last war, for de Gaulle's armoured division?

'Was it not dangerous for a deputy elected by the 'moderates' to demand an alliance with Russia, causing himself to be denounced by André Tardieu in Gringoire as "the friend of the Soviets"?'

The fact that in the 1936 elections I only won my seat in the second Paris arrondissment by a few votes (a constituency where my position had been very strong) shows that in fighting for my country I had accepted the risk of destroying my political career.

De Gaulle is a master of words, but events speak for themselves.

I have never been more convinced of being right than today. This is why I maintain that it is vital to appeal to the French people and to say: it is time you made an effort to understand and to act as a great nation, a free nation, unless you wish to be unworthy of your history.

You were on the right path. You gave your support to men who brought about Franco-German reconciliation by means of Robert Schuman's Coal and Steel Community, and the Common Market, and who, through the Treaty of Rome, gave proof of their desire to create a politically integrated Europe.

The man who fruitlessly opposed this policy, when he came to power, unfortunately remained true to himself.

But by giving him your approval, you have not been true to yourselves. You had supported a policy of solidarity and loyal friendship with the great democracies, who have twice survived the ordeal of blood.

Why have you not been true to yourselves?

This entire policy has been renounced.

France's only chance of political greatness was to create a new Europe alienating all our partners of the Common Market and allowing Germany to usurp the place which should have been France's. You have seen all this and you have said nothing.

You saw France refuse to take part in the discussions in Moscow with Khruschev, Rusk and Macmillan, who signed an agreement which brought hope to the world. France remained aloof and apart in company with Communist China. And you said nothing.

You saw de Gaulle recognise Communist China without previously consulting his allies, in spite of treaty pledges, thus striking a blow against those who are fighting Communism in South-east Asia.

And again you said nothing.

You saw de Gaulle proclaim that he does not wish to be protected by America, upsetting France's traditional policy in order to win support from the uncommitted nations.

It is like some Gallic David whose sling can only inflict scratches on the American Goliath, upon whom his survival depends. Moreover this policy, which divides and weakens the free world, roused the European powers, great and small, against France.

You saw that and you said nothing.

The Constitutional Council, composed almost entirely of the friends of the man in power, decreed, by a crushing majority, that depriving Parliament of the right to legislate by revising the Constitution was to violate the Constitution.

Almost unanimously, with the exception of one vote, the Council of State came to the same conclusion. Yet by a majority of 60% in the referendum of October, 1962, you ratified this violation of the

Constitution . . . This is behaving like people under a dictatorship.
What will your descendants think of you?

Why have you submitted? Because you enjoyed prosperity and because de Gaulle said to you: 'The political stability which you enjoy, you owe to me.' Had you not surrendered, if you were not a nation of 'citizens on strike', you would have known that you owed this prosperity to the Common Market. You would also have known that despite her political instability the Italian nation has profited even more than you from the Common Market.

De Gaulle also said to you: 'If I go it will mean the return of the Fourth Republic,' which he pictured as a 'drunken Helot' with its long line of governments, falling on top of one another.

Untrue! To begin with, in these successive crises de Gaulle played a vital part by getting his followers to vote in Parliament with the Extreme Left and Extreme Right against each government in turn; this he did so systematically that in 1952, when he ordered them to vote against Antoine Pinay, the appointed President of the Council, a revolt broke out within his group in the National Assembly, and split it in two. When offered the Presidency of the Council in 1953, I told the National Assembly that I would not accept the post merely to make a six-month run round the track, and that I would only take it if the majority agreed to modify the Constitution, by providing for an automatic dissolution of the National Assembly should the government be overthrown within eighteen months of its investiture. The Gaullist group voted against me, and I did not form a government.

So much for stability.

As for maintaining that if he relinquished power it would mean a return to the Fourth Republic (with which he periodically threatens us) it is untrue, because the Constitution of the Fourth Republic, which many of us fought from its birth and during its lifetime is, thank God, dead and buried, and no one has any intention of renewing it. Furthermore, to revive it the French would have to vote, and this they do not want to do at any price.

My forthcoming study of the Constitution will show what reforms will have to be put through to ensure that, after de Gaulle, we see governmental stability and parliamentary dignity.

The Constitution gives the French nation the right to elect the Head of State, who boasts today that he enjoys absolute power without being responsible to anyone. The people of France have the right and they have the duty to judge his policies.

The choice of two policies.

Today there is no question of opposing a man who enjoys General de Gaulle's unrivalled reputation.

In such a contest we should be beaten in advance.

It is a question of opposing one political system by another, showing the disastrous effects of the one to which we are subjected at present. There must be respect for the Constitution instead of consent to its daily violation. And the people must be told: 'Dare to make the choice!'

The day the French realise where de Gaulle's policies are leading them, the problem will be solved. Will we then see de Gaulle retire from the political arena? This would certainly spare us the painful spectacle of a gladiatorial contest.

And when, after the French have fought to wipe out the consequences of the mistakes that have been committed, and the situation is back to normal, these same mistakes will be forgotten. It can still be done. Time will have accomplished its work and the name of General de Gaulle will evoke in French hearts only the undying memory of June 18th, 1940.

INDEX